COMPUTER FRIENDLY!

A unique new computer course! Simple…
enjoyable…and above all, understandable!

By Raymond Steinbacher

Printed in U.S.A

All Rights Reserved

Published by Green Tree Press, Inc.

Erie, Pennsylvania 16505

I would like to dedicate this book to all the people behind the curtain who pushed, pulled and helped make this project possible ... and to the person who believes in me the most, my mother.

Raymond Steinbacher

Erie, PA

Introduction

I met Raymond Steinbacher about three years ago. He was a computer software salesperson at our nearby Media Play store. I'd come into the store to get advice about some software.

Since he was selling software, I figured he knew something about it. So I asked him about a program I was considering. Should I download it from a CD-ROM or a floppy? And what was his opinion of the program itself?

Please understand. I hadn't a clue what the word "download" actually meant. And I certainly didn't know the relative merits of CD's vs. floppies.

That's because, as an old typewriter guy, I had a phobic aversion to computers. And, an equally phobic aversion to those very young baggy-panted computer sales clerks who tried to bewilder me with their technical vocabulary.

That was true, until I met Raymond.

Raymond combined the two elements of genuine helpfulness I'd been seeking for years: simple explanations and plain English!

At last! A bright knowledgeable guy who could help me understand how to run my computer!

I asked him if he'd stop by my house and help me with some computer problems. Obviously I offered to pay him (and neither of us was too sure how much that should be).

The price of his visit was a Diet Coke and forty bucks. But, I learned more that evening than I ever had before. From then on, I'd ask him to come over and help me with hardware problems, software problems, internet problems. He even rebuilt my computer from scratch.

It was just a matter of time until I realized that *here* was the *one guy* most qualified to write and develop a *truly basic computer course;* something we'd been wanting to publish here at Green Tree for several years. Because he could explain things more clearly than a dozen computer engineers or scientists. He had the common touch. He could relate to people who, for whatever reason, had been intimidated by their computers. And who had been *even more intimidated* by the books and "tech support" that came with them.

So, this is Raymond's course. He developed it specifically for those of us who see our computers as appliances — not deities from cyberspace!

The course was edited by Floyd Lawrence who worked with Raymond and the crew here at Green Tree. The drawings are by Mark Weber and the page design and layout was administered by Pete Zesinger. By the way, Raymond is now a well respected webmaster and computer consultant.

So, enjoy.

Ernest P. Weckesser, Ph. D.
Green Tree Press, Inc.

Table of Contents

How to use this course

1. This is a very basic course. You probably know some of the material already. Review it anyway. It will help reinforce what you're learning. And, who knows, you may discover some shortcuts and other interesting tidbits you didn't know before.

2. Please do the exercises and other projects as you come across them. Don't allow yourself to think, "Oh, I'll do that later ... another time, maybe." The simple act of doing these projects helps you memorize the material.

3. There is no index. Instead, you'll find a highly detailed Table of Contents. That's because this is a course, not a book. When you wish to refer back to something, you'll find it in context ... not simply on an alphabetized list.

4. Above all, remember that this is a "hands on" course. It's written and designed for a person who's sitting at a computer. So work as you go. Do things. Try things. Have a good time and don't be afraid to make mistakes.

5. We have included a number of pictures within this book. Some of these pictures are small and may be a little difficult to see in detail. These pictures are included within the book only to give you an idea of what your computer screen probably looks like. You should look at your computer screen (and not the small picture within the book) when working in these sections.

Versions of Windows

This book will work with almost all versions of Windows. The newest version is called Windows XP, but this book will also work if you have Windows 2000, Windows Me, Windows 98 or Windows 95. If you don't know which version of Windows you have, don't worry. Just dig into this book and I'm sure you'll be fine. In case you're interested, your computer will usually display a screen when it starts up that tells you which version of Windows you're running.

The newer versions of Windows may run faster and work better on networks (systems of computers that are hooked up to each other), but most of the basic things such as running programs and using the mouse are identical to earlier versions of Windows. To most users, the different versions of Windows will appear very much the same. That's because most of the changes are "under the hood."

I don't think it's necessary for you to upgrade to the newest version of Windows before you read this book. In fact, if you're new to a computer and your computer is now working well, don't change it.

I'd advise waiting to upgrade until you have a good, basic understanding of your computer. Upgrading your computer can open a new can of worms that many times is not worth the trouble.

The point is that for now you don't have to worry about the technical stuff. Just turn the page and start reading this course. You'll be having fun with your computer in no time.

Lesson One

YOUR HARDWARE

Hello. My name is Raymond Steinbacher and I'll be your guide and mentor throughout the course.

Before we begin, I'd like to emphasize that your computer isn't much different from your telephone, your toaster, or your car. All of these are simply tools. They're made for getting things done.

And, for making your life easier ... more productive ... and more enjoyable.

That's what this course is really all about—making your life a little easier. As you read the lessons and follow the simple exercises, you'll gain confidence and knowledge that'll help you use your computer effectively.

I'm assuming that you know nothing about computers. And that's why we're starting with the *basics!*

A computer adds numbers. That's all it does. That may not sound very impressive, but when you can add numbers very quickly, as a computer does, some amazing things are possible. You might enjoy knowing a thing or two about the history of the computer on your desk and how computers worked with numbers in the past.

The earliest computers were very good at generating long lists of numbers without making mistakes. Those original machines were used mostly for computing the many pages of numbers used by scientists in logarithmic calculations. Some of the earliest and most important research is credited to Charles Babbage and George Hunter.

Later in the 20th century, the military used the first modern computers to figure out bomb trajectories. These machines were very slow and very large—some of them as big as a city block. Others took up several floors in an office building. But they were quite good at doing the complex math needed to wage war.

In terms of the work they do, today's computers greatly resemble those early building-sized machines. The inside parts haven't changed all that much. They've just gotten a lot smaller and they operate a lot faster.

In fact, the computer you have today is faster and more powerful than the multi-million-dollar computers of the 1970s and early 1980s. With all this power at your fingertips, you'll find it easy to get real enjoyment from your computer. This course will lead you to that enjoyment—quickly and simply.

You'll learn how to use a computer to communicate with other people. Or, if you'd like, you can research your family history, learn more about health and medicine, or discover fantastic bargains all over the world.

Besides the entertainment and information you'll get, you can also use your computer for work. After completing my course, you might even decide to earn a living with your computer by working from your home. Thousands of people have done it. And more people are doing it every day.

No matter what your reasons are for using a computer, it'll quickly become the most useful appliance in your home. After finishing the course, you'll keep on discovering new uses for it. The possibilities are truly endless.

First, let me acquaint you with the basic parts of a computer. This way you'll become familiar with some of the common terms people use when they talk about computers.

A Basic Computer

Here are the simple parts on your computer. These parts are commonly known as hardware.

Cards

These are little boards made of plastic that connect or plug into the Motherboard. They are small, specialized little computers that each do a different job. Sometime you may have to connect cables and other things into a card. Connecting cables into a card is often called plugging into the card. Just like you plug a lamp into an electrical outlet, you plug your speakers into the sound card.

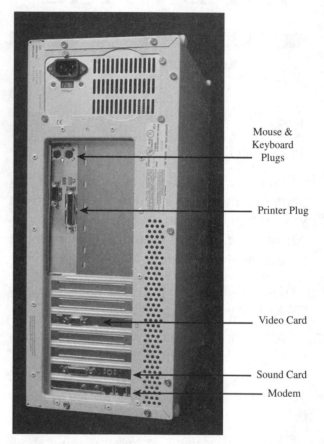

Mouse & Keyboard Plugs

Printer Plug

Video Card

Sound Card

Modem

Back of the computer

CD-ROM

This looks like an ordinary CD-ROM you'd use to play music. But these store programs.

CD ROM and CD Drive

Disk Drive and Floppy Disk

CD-ROM Drive

This is where you put the CD-ROM you want to use. It opens when you press the button on the front. When the tray comes out, place the CD on it, silver side down. Then push the tray back into the computer—very gently, please. On most CD-ROM Drives, pressing the button will also close the tray automatically.

CPU

This is The "Central Processing Unit." Everything that happens on the computer goes through the CPU before you see or hear what's happened. CPU's come in different speeds and models.

Disk Drive

This is the small slot on the front of your computer with a button under it. You insert "Floppy disks" into it. To retrieve the disk, just press the button.

Floppy

These are flat, square things that look a bit like plastic coasters with a metal center. They're used to save the things you do on your computer. You can then take the floppy (or "disk" as it's sometimes called) and put it into someone else's computer in order to share your work and projects with them. Floppy disks are actually rigid, not floppy.

Hard Drive

This is like a much larger floppy, except that you can't see it or take it out of your computer. It's built into the computer case and stores all the information needed to run your computer.

Keyboard

This looks a lot like a typewriter keyboard, and it also works just like one. Just strike the letters or numbers you want and they show up on the computer screen.

Microphone

You may or may not have a microphone with your computer. If you do, it plugs into the "Sound Card" receptacle on the back of your computer. You can use it to record sounds.

With the right programs, you can use the microphone to speak into your computer. It'll then do your typing for you.

Modem

The modem makes the connection with the Internet. Plug it into the telephone jack on the wall where your phone is normally plugged. The phone then plugs into the back of the modem. The other end of the modem plugs into a receptacle on the back of the computer. This is the ordinary hookup for modems that are separate boxes made to sit either upon or next to the computer. Most modems, though, are built right into the computer. Even so, you still need to connect the modem to a phone jack in your home. Some modems can also be used as fax machines. Others can even be used as a voice mail system. More about modems when we cover the Internet.

Monitor

This is what looks just like your television set. And works almost exactly the same way. The main difference is that its special cord plugs into the back of your computer. It also has better picture quality than most television sets.

Motherboard

Everything inside your computer—the "CPU," the "Sound Card," everything—plugs into this big, flat board that's also inside. I think of this as the backbone of the computer.

Mouse

This is the little hand-held device you roll around on a mouse pad. It has two or sometimes three buttons on it, a small ball in the bottom of it, and a long wire coming out of it that plugs into the back of the computer. You'll use a mouse to move things around on the computer screen and to give commands to the computer.

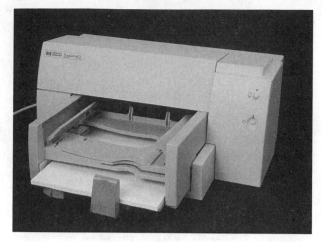

A Printer

Printer

A printer may or may not have been included with your computer system. You put paper into it and it prints the work you've done on the computer onto the paper. You might be able to print in color too. If you're not sure whether you can, take a quick look to see if your printer has the word "color" somewhere on the front of its case.

Programs

A program is the term used for anything special your computer does for you. There are programs that enable you to do just about anything—from playing games to making posters. Most likely you have some programs already installed in your computer. You can also go to a computer store and buy them. Most people call programs "Software."

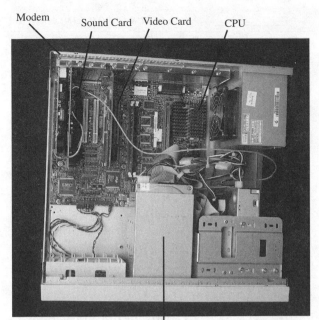

Modem Sound Card Video Card CPU

Hard Disk

Inside Your Computer

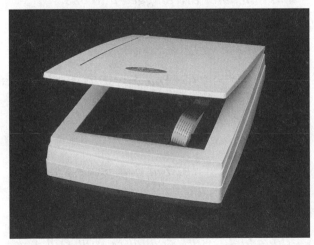

Scanner

Scanner

You may not have gotten a scanner with your computer system. I look at it as a camera for the computer. You place things on the glass surface of the scanner, close the lid, and the scanner then takes a picture that shows up on your computer. More about how to use a scanner later in the course.

Software

This is a fancy name for "Programs." Some software comes with your computer, and you can buy more at computer stores. You can find software to do thousands of jobs. Browse

around next time you're out shopping.

Sound card: This is one of the little boards that plugs into the motherboard. It's the part that makes all the sounds you hear when you're using the computer. Sound cards today have very high sound quality, matching or even exceeding what you hear coming from an expensive stereo system. This is the card that enables you to play a music CD on your computer. The speakers and a microphone all plug into this card.

Speakers

These are much like the ones you have on your stereo, but probably a little more compact. They make the sounds and play the music you hear from your computer. Some speakers are built right into your monitor. Others are separate.

Video Card

Your monitor plugs into a video card. It's the part of the computer that puts up the images you see on the screen and makes the pictures move.

Word Processor

This is a specialized program used to create letters and other typed documents. You might say it turns your computer into a high-tech typewriter. The more expensive word processors can help you with spelling and grammar.

Take some time to review these terms. Look at the picture to see where the parts of your computer are located. Soon you'll begin to feel comfortable with it. Then, later on in the course, when I refer to something you'll know what it is and what it's used for.

That's all there really is to your computer. Sure, lots of other complex things are going on inside. But you don't need to know anything technical to use and enjoy a computer. After all, many people use and enjoy cars every day, but not many are actual mechanics.

Viruses

A virus is a special type of program that is meant to cause your computer to do something bad. Some viruses can wipe out all the information on your computer and others are like an April Fools' joke and make strange or annoying messages appear on your screen. You can get viruses by sharing disks or programs with friends or you can get them by downloading files or programs off of the Internet. There are special programs you can buy that will help you find and remove any viruses you may have on your computer. See viruses section in Lesson 5 for more info.

Exercise #1
Enter the correct word

_____ 1. *Little boards that make your computer do more things. They plug into the Motherboard.*

_____ 2. *A special program that lets you type letters and other documents.*

_____ 3. *This drive is where you put the silver disks into.*

_____ 4. *This looks like your television set and gives you information about what the computer is doing.*

_____ 5. *Small flat, squares that you use to store programs or files on.*

_____ 6. *The built-in disk that stores all the programs and files that make your computer work.*

_____ 7. *The heart of your computer. It is the brain that makes everything work.*

_____ 8. *The part of the computer that you type with.*

_____ 9. *Stores programs and music. They can be silver or gold colored. You put these in your computer.*

_____ 10. *This is a special board that plugs into your computer. The speakers plug into this board as well as a microphone.*

_____ 11. *If you have one attached to your computer, you can record sounds into your computer with it.*

_____ 12. *The part of your computer that gets plugged into the telephone line.*

_____ 13. *This is the main board of your computer. All the other parts of your computer are plugged into this.*

_____ 14. *Another word for software. These make your computer do things.*

_____ 15. *You buy this for your computer at stores. This makes your computer do new things. Another word for programs.*

_____ 16. *You can place pictures in this device and put them in a computer.*

_____ 17. *If you have one of these attached to your computer you can get copies of your letters and make flyers.*

_____ 18. *These are the parts of the computer that make the sounds you hear.*

_____ 19. *This is the small card that the monitor is plugged into.*

_____ 20. *A small slot on the front of your computer. You put floppy disks into it.*

_____ 21. *You can use this device to move your electronic finger (pointer) around the screen and give the computer commands.*

Lesson Two

GETTING STARTED

Before you turn your computer on, make sure you have a good, high-quality surge protector with at least a U.L. rating. It should have a telephone line input and output on it too. Plug the various components from your computer into the receptacles on the surge protector. Then plug the surge protector into a wall receptacle. This protects your computer from damage if there's a lightning storm or a power surge.

In fact, if you really want to protect your system you should buy a battery backup for your computer. These systems, which are called uninterruptible power supplies (UPS), give you much more protection than a regular surge protector. If the power goes out, the uninterruptible power supply will power your computer. You'll have time to shut down your computer the proper way before the battery runs out.

Make sure the surge protector's "on/off" switch is in the "on" position.

Now it's time to turn your computer on. First, make sure you don't have any floppy disks in the drives. Eject them by pressing

the small button next to the disk slot. A floppy disk left in its slot can often times keep a computer from starting properly.

Make sure everything is plugged in and ready to go. First, turn the monitor on by pressing its power button. Then, if your speakers have their own power switch, turn that on. Finally, turn the computer on. Several things will begin to happen. Just relax and watch the show. Turning your computer on is called "booting" the computer.

First you'll see a black screen with some text on it. Your computer then runs a self-test, and you'll see numbers counting up very quickly. After that you may hear a beep from your computer and then see some other screens.

Next a Windows screen comes on. A moving bar across the bottom of your screen, or some other animation lets you know that Windows is loading. The screen may flash off and on a bit, and you may see some words on the screen. This is normal, so just keep waiting.

You'll know that Windows has finished loading when your monitor's "desktop" displays the "My Computer" and "Recycle Bin" icons — the Windows XP desktop may only show the "Recycle Bin" icon.

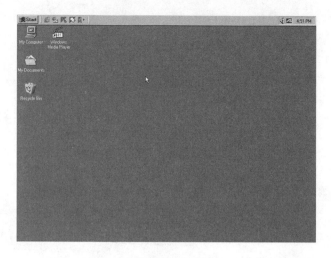

A Desktop

Now you're ready to go.

If you see a window that asks you how to boot and displays a list of options, choose number one — "Normal Boot." This can happen if the computer was turned off improperly. For now, don't worry about it.

If you just can't seem to get your computer past this point, or if the Windows screen doesn't appear, you may have a problem. Contact the person who sold you the computer and describe the sequence of events. Your computer may have been altered in some way.

The real trick to learning about your computer is just to play with it. It's vital that you get as much hands-on experience with your machine as you can. Your successful completion of the course depends upon this. Don't worry about hurting the computer. It can tolerate any of your mistakes.

This is a self-teaching course, so move along at your own pace. If you don't understand something, just go back, try it again, and then again if necessary. If you don't own your own computer, you may be able to use one at a friend's house or perhaps at the local library.

Exercise #2
Choose the correct answer

1. *How will you know when Windows has finished loading?*

   a. *A big window that has the Microsoft logo on it appears.*

   b. *You will see the desktop with the "My Computer" and the "Recycle Bin".*

   c. *The hard disk will stop making noise.*

2. *What kind of surge protector should you buy?*

   a. *One with lots of plugs on it and a power button.*

   b. *One from the hardware store.*

   c. *One with at least a U.L. rating and telephone line protection.*

3. *Should you have a floppy disk in your drive when you boot your computer?*

   a. *Yes, it is needed to boot the computer.*

   b. *No, it could interfere with the normal boot process of your computer.*

   c. *Only if you want to install programs.*

4. *If you should see a message with a list on it asking you how to boot your computer what should you do?*

   a. *Choose number one, Normal Boot.*

   b. *Turn your computer off.*

   c. *Call for help.*

Lesson Three

WELCOME TO WINDOWS

Windows is a big program that's called an "operating system." It's the master program that runs all the other programs you use on your computer. It's also the program you use to give your computer instructions and to make it do things.

In order to get the most out of your computer, it's important that you understand the key parts of the Windows operating system. There are lots of parts, but don't worry. Windows was designed to be both easy and highly visual. Play with it a bit as you continue this lesson. You'll find that you're soon picking up the basics of how to get around in Windows very quickly.

By the way, for now you can consider Windows 95, 98, 2000, Windows Me and Windows XP to be the same. Whenever any significant differences between them need to be explained, I'll do so at that time.

I.
Windows
Terminology

Imagine that you're sitting at an electronic desk. When your computer starts up and no programs are running, you'll see what's called the "desktop." On the desktop you'll see some little pictures. These are called "icons."

On every Windows desktop is an icon called "My Computer." The only exception is Windows XP and I'll show you how to put the "My Computer" icon on your desktop later in this section. It resembles a computer. Another icon is labeled "Recycle Bin." This one looks like a trash can. There may be other icons on your desktop, and it's possible that your pictures of the trash can or computer may look a bit different from the ones shown in the photo. But you'll recognize them by the identifying words beneath them. Later you'll learn how to change the pictures of these icons and how to customize your desktop to meet your own needs.

Another object on your computer screen looks like a little arrow. It'll be at the very center of your screen if you haven't touched the mouse after turning on the computer.

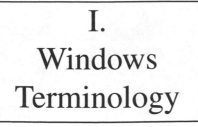

19

It's called the "pointer." Think of it as an electronic finger you use for pointing to things on the screen.

The pointer is attached to the mouse. So, when you move the mouse, the pointer moves too. The pointer is important because it tells you where on the computer screen your electronic finger is pointing.

You can use the mouse to point to things like programs or folders. You do this by moving the pointer on top of an icon. By then clicking the left button on the mouse, you can tell the computer to run the program or open the folder. You'll learn more on this topic later.

You'll also see what's called a "task bar" on your desktop. It's a light gray bar that's usually at the bottom or the top of the screen. It can also be moved to the sides. You'll know you're looking at the task bar when you see the "Start" button at one end and the clock at the other end.

Start	12:40 PM

Task Bar

The task bar can be hidden from view or moved around the screen. You'll learn how to do these things later on. If you don't see the task bar, it might be hidden. You can find it by using the mouse to move the pointer all the way to the edge of the screen. You may have to try all four sides to find it. But when the pointer bumps into it, the task bar jumps out and becomes visible. After you move the mouse pointer off the task bar, it'll automatically disappear again.

If your task bar is hidden, find it and try to remember where it is. If you ever forget where you left it, you can always find it by moving the pointer to the edges of the screen.

Find the task bar. Place the pointer on top of the clock. What happens?

The date will appear if you leave the pointer over the clock.

With the left mouse button, click once on the "Start" button. Look at the list that appears. When you're done, simply click on the "Start" button again with the left mouse button and the list will go away.

Exercise #3
Complete the following

1. *Windows is an* _____.

2. *The little pictures you see on the desktop are called* _____.

3. *The little arrow that is your electronic finger is the* _____.

4. *How can you tell you are looking at the taskbar? What two things will be visible* _____

In Windows, just about every program you run will appear on your screen as a small rectangular box called a window. Either a name or information inside the window tells you what program you're running. The program will also appear on the task bar.

Become familiar with the following parts of a window. Don't worry if you don't understand them yet. Just get to know where these parts are.

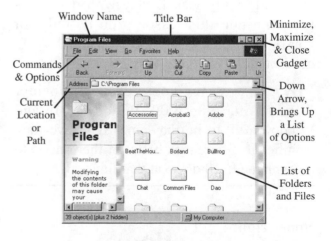

An Example Window

Application: This is simply another name for a program.

Open: This means to begin running a program.

Close: This means to quit or exit a program. When you close a window, it disappears from the desktop. You can close any window by clicking on the X in the upper right hand corner of the window you want to close. This will also close any program that's running inside the window.

Drag: Place the pointer over an icon by moving the mouse. Press the left button and hold it down. While holding the left button down, move the mouse and watch the icon move with it. You're literally dragging the icon around the screen. When you move the icon to where you want it, release the mouse button. I'll give you a practice session later.

Double Click: Quickly press down twice on the left mouse button. You should hear the button click each time you press it. If you don't click twice quickly enough, the computer won't know what you want to do. Look for the practice session later.

Execute: This simply means to run a program or launch an application.

File: A file can be either a program or a part of a program. As you might suppose, a file contains information you've generated. If you've created a letter in a word processor and have saved it, the saved letter is called a file.

Folder: Files are kept inside folders. In fact, your computer stores information much as you would store it in a file cabinet.

Gadget: A gadget is small icon that's used to make something happen on your screen. Good examples are the "Close" gadget in the upper right-hand corner of a window (it's an "X"), or the "Scroll bar" in a window.

Pointer: The pointer, you might recall, is your electronic finger that's controlled by the mouse. We've covered this before, but it

bears repeating. The pointer is usually shaped like an arrow, but it can change into other shapes as you run programs. For example, if your computer is busy working on a task, the pointer will change into an hourglass, letting you know that you should wait until the computer is done. As you go through this course, you'll get to know the different shapes the pointer can take.

Exercise #4
Complete the following

1. *An organizational tool used to structure the way you save files on your computer is called a* _____ .

2. *To begin running a program you* _____.

3. *Clicking on an icon and holding the mouse button down while you move the mouse will* _____.

4. *A quick pressing of the mouse button twice is called* _____.

5. *A word that means to run a program is* _____.

6. *To quit or exit a program you* _____.

7. *A collection of information you save on your hard disk or floppy disk is a* _____.

8. *A fancy name for a program is* _____.

Input: This is a verb meaning to place information into your computer. For instance, your computer could ask you a question such as "What's your name?" If you respond by typing your name, you're inputting.

Install: When you put a new program on your computer, you're installing it. And that enables you to run it.

Launch: This means to run or execute a program, or to start using an application.

21

Left Click: This means pressing the left mouse button with your finger and releasing it. You'll get the hang of this the more you use your mouse.

Load: You may want to continue a project you're working on at a later time. To begin where you left off, you'll need to load the project into the program you're using. For example, if you're writing a letter and you decide to finish it later, you could "load" your half-finished letter and then finish it.

Maximize: To maximize means to enlarge any window so that it fills up your entire desktop. The maximize gadget is located on every window in the upper right hand corner. It's the middle gadget that looks like an empty desktop. Once you click this button to make the window fill the screen, the icon changes into two overlapping windows. The gadget has now changed into the restore button.

Minimize: This is the small icon in the upper right corner of every window, next to the maximize and close gadgets. If you press the minimize gadget, it seems to make the window disappear. If you look at your task bar, though, you'll see a small rectangle with the name of the window or program you just minimized. If you left click once on the rectangle the window will return to the size it was before you minimized it. This is a handy feature for getting at something on the desktop behind the window you're working on. Just minimize the window and do whatever you needed to do on your desktop. To return to the window you minimized, just click on the appropriate rectangle in the taskbar to reopen it.

Exercise #5
Complete the following

1. A small tool used to make things happen on your screen. The X in the upper right hand corner of a window is an example of this _____.

2. Putting information into your computer is called _____.

3. The word that means to put a new program on your computer or to place a new piece of hardware on your system is _____.

4. Another fancy word that means to run or start using an application is _____.

5. Pressing and releasing the left mouse button once is called _____.

6. The word that means to get information you saved before and use it with a program at a later time is _____.

7. Making a window as big as it can get is called to _____.

8. To make a window as small as it can get is called to _____.

Menu: A menu is just that—a list of things you can order. In the world of computers, a menu is a list of commands and options you can give a computer.

Restore: The restore gadget is essentially the same as the maximize button. It's the middle gadget in the upper right corner of a window. It looks like two overlapping windows. If you click on this button, the maximized window will go back to its original size. Then this button changes back into the maximize gadget and looks like a single window.

Right Click: This means pressing the right mouse button with your finger and releasing it. You need to click the right button only once.

Run: This just means to start something on the computer. When you double click on a program to start it, you're running a program.

Save: This means to put your work onto a floppy or hard disk so you can retrieve it and use it later.

Scroll bar: On the right side and along the bottom of some windows is a slider with arrows at each end. These are "Scroll bars." Place your pointer on either the vertical bar or the horizontal bar and drag it up and down or side to side. If there's a very big picture on your screen that won't all fit in a window, scroll bars will appear. You can then click on the arrows to view other parts of the image.

Horizontal Scroll Bar

Shortcut: A logical name for a bookmark to a file or a program you use a lot. For example, if you were working on a letter, you could create a shortcut to that file on your desktop. The next time you wanted to work on the letter, you could simply double click on the shortcut to start the word processor and load the file all in one step.

Exercise #6
Supply the correct term

1. To store work on a floppy or hard disk for later use. _____

2. The middle gadget in the upper right hand corner of a window. It looks like two overlapping windows. _____

3. Using your finger to press down and release the right button on the mouse.

_____

4. On the right side and along the bottom of some windows the slider with arrows on each end. _____

5. A list of options or commands you can give your computer. _____

6. To start something on your computer.

_____

7. A quick way to get to a program or a file you use a lot. _____

Shut Down: You do this every time you're ready to shut your computer off. It's the last option in the list that appears when you left click once on the start button in the task bar.

Start Button: This is labeled "Start" on the task bar. Use this button to start programs, to perform many important tasks on the computer, and to shut the computer off.

Task Bar: This is the bar containing the start button and the clock. It shows you what tasks or programs you're running by placing them in small rectangular boxes. You can quickly switch from program to program or window to window by clicking on the appropriate box in the task bar. If nothing's showing in the task bar, you can assume that no programs are running, or that no files or folders are open.

Title Bar: This appears at the top of each window and contains the name of that particular window. Usually the computer puts inside the title bar the name of the program or file that's being displayed in the window. Moving a window is easy. Just place the pointer over the title bar, click on the left mouse button and hold it down, and then drag the window anywhere on your desktop. Notice the minimize, maximize and close gadgets at the far right of the title bar.

Window: A box that appears as you run or open things on your computer is called a window. Everything you do happens in a window.

Study these terms and the accompanying diagrams to get a feel for what a window looks like and where the important buttons and gadgets are.

Exercise #7
Complete the following

1. Boxes that appear as you run or open things on your computer are called _____.

2. The process you must go through to turn your computer off is called _____.

3. The bar with the clock that shows you what your computer is running is the _____.

4. The main button on the taskbar is the _____.

5. This is the area at the top of each window that has the name of the program you are using. _____.

Mouse Pointers

The different kinds of pointers or cursors on your screen give you needed information about what options you have at a given moment.

Here are some examples:

• **Arrow:** This is the standard pointer used to point to things on the desktop.

• **Double arrow:** This pointer can be a vertical double-headed arrow, a horizontal double-headed arrow, or a double-headed arrow on an angle. This pointer generally means that you can click and drag the window edge to make the window larger or smaller.

• **Hourglass:** When you see this, it means that your computer is busy working on something. You'll often see the hourglass just after you run a program. It's the computer's way of asking you to wait until the program has started.

• **Cursor, vertical bar:** You'll frequently see this when you're using a word processor, or inputting information into the computer with the keyboard. This is called a cursor. It's usually blinking. It means that the computer is waiting for you to type something. Letters or numbers will appear from this blinking cursor as you type. It is also the insertion point when you are pasting text in your word processing programs.

Exercise # 8
Match the correct term

1. The standard pointer that you use to point to things on the desktop.

_____

2. This pointer generally means that you can click and drag the window edge making the window larger or smaller.

_____

3. This means that your computer is busy working on something. _____

_____

4. Usually this is for inputting information into the computer. _____

⧗	⇖	⤢	I
a.	b.	c.	d.

5. Name the parts of this window ....

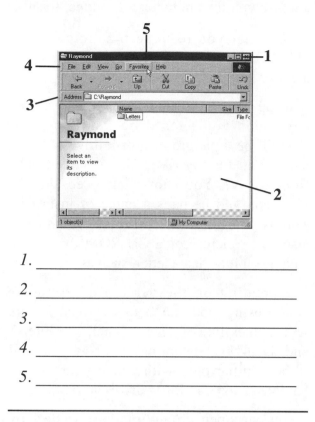

1. _____

2. _____

3. _____

4. _____

5. _____

Look at the Windows desktop. You should see some icons on it as well as in the task bar. Remember, you can easily identify the task bar by the "Start" button in one corner and the clock in the other. The task bar runs across the entire edge of the screen.

The task bar will always be on one of the four edges of your monitor. If you can't see it, then it's probably hidden. You can find it by moving the pointer all the way up to the top of the desktop. Then push up a bit more, just as though you're trying to move the pointer off of the screen.

If that doesn't work try the same technique with each of the other sides of the screen bottom, left and right. When you do locate it, remember where it is. Later you'll learn how to turn the hiding taskbar on and off. For now, just leave it as it is.

Now take another look at the desktop. You're looking for an icon named "My Computer" that's usually sitting in the upper left corner of the desktop. It might be in another location. When you find it, put the pointer on top of it.

My Computer

Note Window XP users: If you don't see a "My Computer" icon on your desktop and you're using Windows XP follow these steps.

1. Right click on an empty area of the desktop, be sure not to right click on the taskbar or the Start button.

2. Choose "Properties" from the list that appears.

3. Click on the "Desktop" tab near the top of the Display Properties windows that opens.

4. Near the bottom of the screen find the button labeled "Customize Desktop" and click on it.

5. Make sure there is a checkmark next to the "My Documents" and "My Computer" options. If there isn't a checkmark place one there by clicking on the empty box to the left of the options.

6. Click on the "OK" button and then again on the 'OK' button in the other window.

You should now see a "My Computer" and "My Documents" icon on your desktop. If you don't then go back through the steps to make sure you didn't miss anything.

Now left click **once**. The icon and the words "My Computer" should become darker, probably with a bluish shading. That means that you've "selected" this icon.

Now move the pointer over the "Recycle Bin" icon. Left click on it **once**. Now the "My Computer" icon is no longer selected. Instead, the "Recycle Bin" is now selected. Put the pointer back over the "My Computer" icon and select it again with a single left click of the mouse button.

Recycle Bin

"My Computer" is a special icon that will let you see and use certain parts of your computer. To open and see what's inside "My Computer," you need to tell Windows you'd like to do that. You do this by **double** clicking. While holding the pointer on top of the "My Computer" icon, click the left mouse button **twice**.

You may have to experiment with the speed you use in clicking the button. Click too quickly and it may not work. Click too slowly and nothing will happen. So if you don't see anything the first time, try clicking at slightly different speeds. You can't hurt anything by practicing,

When you do the clicking correctly, a window opens up. Inside it, you'll see some more icons. They should look something like this.

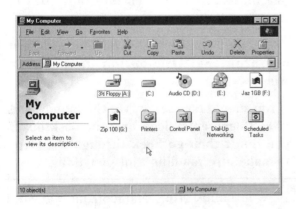

Icons in a window

For now, just find the "Close" gadget in the upper right corner of the window. It's the one with an "X" inside. Left click on it once. The window will disappear. Now practice double clicking on the "My Computer" icon. Open the window. Then close it. Practice that

for a few moments. This maneuver is used a lot, so you'll want to get a good feel for it.

Now that you're done practicing, open "My Computer" and leave it open. Let's take a closer look at this window.

In the "My Computer" window are a few key icons you should be familiar with. There'll be a picture of a disk drive with the name 3.5" Floppy (A:). This is called your floppy drive. You should also see another disk icon and perhaps a name or just "C:." This is your internal hard drive. You should also see a picture of a CD-ROM drive with a name on it or just a letter, such as "D:."

Depending on the version of Windows you're using, you may also see some folders with names like "Control Panel," "Printers" and "Dial-Up Networking." For now, you need to be familiar only with where your floppy, hard disk, and CD-ROM drives are.

You can open up any of these folders by double clicking on them just as you did to open up the "My Computer" icon. The only exception is that you can't open up the floppy or CD-ROM drives unless something is in them. So if you click on a CD-ROM drive and get an error telling you that the "Drive is not accessible," just click "Cancel." The same holds true for the floppy drive. If there's no disk in there, when you double click on it you'll get a message saying "Drive is not accessible. Error." Don't worry. Just click cancel.

Windows names every drive on your computer by placing a letter next to it followed by a colon (:). So the first drive, the floppy, is usually designated "A: drive." If you have a second floppy drive, it'll be called "B: drive." Your internal hard drive is called "C:." Then the CD-ROM drive and any other drives you may have on your system would be named accordingly.

You can name your hard drive (or disk) anything you want, but it will still have a "(C:)" at the end of the name. This is because Windows always calls your hard drive the "(C:)" drive. The CD-ROM will have different names for each CD you put into it, but it will always have the Windows letter following the name.

So a computer with one floppy, one hard disk and one CD-ROM drive would have the following window names:

• A: Floppy disk drive

• C: Hard disk drive

• D: CD-ROM drive

Exercise #9
Answer the following questions

1. How do you select an icon, file or folder?

_____

_____

2. If you want to open a folder or run a program, how do you do that?

_____

3. What letter does windows give to your internal hard drive? _____

4. What is the letter name windows gives to your floppy drive? _____

From time to time you'll come across a manual or a program that asks you to "Place a disk in the A: drive" or a CD into the "D: drive" and then to "Press enter." So you need to know what the letters of your drives are. Make a note of the drives you have and write their letter names on a sheet for future reference.

Now, open up your hard disk by double clicking on the C: drive. You'll notice that it contains even more files and folders. If you're wondering what the difference is between a file and a folder, just remember that something is a folder if it has a yellow folder icon next to its name.

Note: If you're using Windows XP and you get a screen that warns you about viewing the contents of the drive, click on the "show files" option.

Think of this as a filing system. If you wanted to, you could simply put all your files on the hard disk and not have any folders at all. But that practice could soon lead to an inefficient mess. Can you imagine looking for your resume or some tax information by sifting through 20,000 other files on the hard disk? It would take forever.

Files will have other types of icons next to their name depending on what type they are. A folder can hold as many files as you want, and you can create as many folders as you want. This is the standard way that Windows organizes the material on any of your drives.

Now find a folder on your C: drive and double click on it. You'll see even more files, maybe some folders, too. Depending on what folder you pick, you may find many levels of folders inside folders. Don't let that throw you.

It would be wise to create a folder on the hard disk called "taxes." Then, inside the taxes folder you could create a "federal taxes" folder. That's where you'd put everything related to federal income taxes and the Internal Revenue Service. To work on federal taxes, all you'd have to do is open the "taxes" folder by double clicking on it. Then you'd find the "federal taxes" folder, double click on it, and you'd have the information you need to begin working. You should learn to do this with anything you wish to file.

By now you might have a lot of windows open. That's okay. Just close them all by clicking on the "Close" gadget in the upper right-hand corner of each window. Close all the windows now so that you see only the desktop.

II.
The Basic Features of Windows

By this time, you should know how to move the mouse, how to click and double click, and how to open folders. In this section you'll be learning about the basic parts of a window, as well as how to use scroll bars and resize a window.

1. Double click on the "My Computer" icon.

2. Find the C: drive (your hard disk) and double click on it.

3. Now find the folder called "Program Files" and double click on it. If you don't have this folder, just open another folder. But don't open the Windows folder at this time.

If other windows are open don't worry. We'll be using just this one window for now.

Move your pointer over the top of the maximize gadget. If you're not sure where that is, you should refer back to the list of terms. Left click on it and notice what happens. The window got very large.

Click on the maximize gadget again. And notice what happens. The window went back to its original size.

When you clicked on the maximize gadget, the window filled the entire screen. When you clicked on it again, the window returned to its original size. This is a handy button to use if you've got too much information in a window for all of it to be visible. By clicking on the maximize button to make the window larger, you can then see more of the material that's in the window. Then you can click again on the maximize button to return to the window's original size.

Clicking on the maximize button can have two results:

1. If the window is **not** full size, this will make it full size.

2. If the window is already full size, this will make the window go back to a smaller size.

In fact, when the window isn't full size, the middle gadget is called the maximize gadget. But if the window's already full size, you'll notice that the gadget now looks different—sort of like two overlapping windows. This is referred to as the "Restore" gadget because it's used to restore the window to its original size.

Now place the pointer over the minimize button and left click on it. The window will shrink and seem to disappear. If you also had another window open, you'll now see that window. If you didn't have any other window open, you'll see the desktop. It's just like picking something up off your desk, putting it somewhere else, and seeing what was beneath it on the surface of the desk.

Now look at the task bar. You'll see a rectangle with a folder and the words "Program Files" (or words naming whatever folder you had opened).

If you've got more than one window open, you may see other rectangles in the task bar. Don't worry about them yet.

Move your pointer directly over the rectangle in the taskbar and left click on it. Doing this brings the file window back to your screen, all ready for you to work on again.

Try using the minimize button when the window is full size and then when it's not full size. Notice any difference?

No, because the minimize button has the same effect on any size window. It'll always reduce the window to a rectangle in the taskbar.

Now place the pointer on the "Close" gadget, the one with the "X" in it. Left click once. You'll notice that the window vanishes. Even the task bar shows no trace of it. That's because you've closed the window — as opposed to merely reducing it as you do with the minimize gadget. Once again, if you've got another window open beneath the window you just closed, it'll now be visible.

Now I'd like you to find the "Program Files" folder again and open it up.

Make sure that the window isn't maximized. Do this by checking the middle gadget in the upper right-hand corner. It should look like one window, not two overlapping windows.

Now move the pointer to the bottom right corner of the window. Your cursor should change into a double-headed arrow. See the figure below. If your pointer doesn't change, move it around the corner a bit until it does. Be sure you're moving the pointer around in the lower right hand corner of the folder's window, not in the corner of the monitor's screen.

Once you see the double-headed arrow pointer, press and hold down the left mouse button. Move the mouse around. You're dragging the corner of the window around and resizing it. When you have the window to a size you want, release your finger from the mouse button.

Try doing this a few times until you get the hang of it.

You can also resize just one side of the window. All you do is move the pointer to the left, right, bottom or top border of a window.

Move the pointer to the edge of a window very slowly. Just as the pointer is about to go outside the window border and onto the desktop underneath, it'll change into a double-headed arrow. Hold the mouse

right there. Now you can click and drag that side of a window. Release the mouse button when you get the window to the size you want. You can do this on any side or any corner of the window.

Here's how to move the whole window without changing its shape. Move the pointer over the title bar, the area of the window where the words "Program Files" appear. They'll be different words if you've opened a different folder. Click and hold down the left mouse button. Now drag the window with the mouse. Notice that the entire window moves. When you're done repositioning the window on your desktop, just release the mouse button.

Exercise #10
Practice the following

• *Open a folder and make it very wide by resizing the right or the left side of the window.*

• *Now make it very tall by resizing the window at the top or the bottom of the window.*

• *Grab the window at one of the corners and then resize it back to a smaller window size.*

Practice both moving and resizing your "Program Files" folder. When you're done, make the window rather small, about four inches square. When you do this, you'll see scroll bars at the side and bottom of the window.

You're now looking at the contents of the folder through a small window. Imagine that you cut a four-inch square hole in the middle of a piece of paper and then placed the paper over a newspaper page. You'd be able to see only a small part of the newspaper through the square hole.

In many ways, this is what you're doing with windows. The window is the paper with the hole in it, and the material inside the window is the newspaper. If you wanted to read the whole paper, you'd have to move the hole around over the newspaper. The whole newspaper is there, but you just can't see it all.

The same thing happens with windows. You've made a small window, so you can't see everything in the folder through that window. The scrollbars enable you to move the little paper with the hole (the window) up, down, left and right so that you can see the whole page underneath.

There are three main parts to a scroll bar.

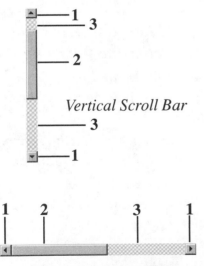

Vertical Scroll Bar

Horizontal Scroll Bar

1 — arrows on each end of the scroll bar.

2 — a square or rectangular gadget between the two arrows that you can "grab" and move with your cursor.

3 — a light gray area between the arrows.

In your "Program Files" window, put your pointer over the arrow pointing down in the right side scroll bar. Left click on it once. You'll see the contents in the little window move up one line.

Likewise, if you click once on the up arrow at the top of the scroll bar, the contents inside the window will move down one line at a time.

Now try clicking once with the left mouse button on the right-pointing arrow in the bottom scroll bar. You'll see the contents in the window move off to the left. If you click once on the left-pointing arrow at the other end of the scroll bar, the contents will scroll to the right.

You can also hold the mouse button down on any of these scroll bar arrows. In that case, the contents keep scrolling until you release the mouse button.

In addition, you can scroll around by using the scroll gadget. If you put your mouse pointer on top of the rectangle inside the scroll bar on the right side, then click on it and drag it up or down, you'll see the contents move up or down. When you've moved up or down as far as you want, release the mouse button. You can do the same thing with the rectangle in the bottom scroll bar, using it to move the contents of the window left or right.

Finally, if you put the pointer in the light gray area of the scroll bar just above, below, to the left, or to the right of a scroll bar arrows and click, the window will scroll more quickly.

Take some time to play with the scrollbars. And practice resizing windows. These are steps you'll be using often, and you should feel comfortable with them.

There's one more item on the Windows desktop that you should be aware of. It's called the task bar, and it provides you with various information. By looking at it, you can tell the time of day, as well as what programs are running or what windows are open.

Make sure you don't have any programs open. Close any that are. Now look at the task bar. The area between the "Start" button and the clock should be mostly—if not completely—blank.

Double click on the "My Computer" icon. You'll see the window open, and you'll also see that a new box appears on the task bar. This is a quick way to let you know that a window is open.

Now minimize the window. It'll disappear from the desktop, but it'll still be visible on the task bar. That's because the window is really still open, even though you just made it disappear. If you click on the box in the task bar labeled "My Computer," the window will open up again. Go ahead and try this.

If you're using Windows 98, Windows 2000, or Windows XP there's an additional feature that you don't have in Windows 95. Leave the "My Computer" window open. The label in the task bar will look pushed in. If you put the pointer over that label and click on it, the task bar button will pop out and the window will automatically minimize.

A. Date and time

If you want to change the time or date on the task bar, you can do it quickly by placing the mouse pointer over the clock and double clicking.

A new window will open up showing a wall clock and a calendar. To change the date, follow these steps.

1. Select the month by clicking on the down pointing arrow at the end of the month. When you do this a drop down list appears. Click the desired month.

2. To set the year, click on the small up or down arrows at the end of the year box.

3. Then click once on the day of the month in the calendar below the month and year.

To set the time, do the following.

1. Below the clock is a printout of the time. Put the pointer on top of the hour and left click. Now scroll with the up or down

arrows on the side of the time box to make adjustments to the hour.

2. Put the pointer over the minutes and left click. Scroll up or down again to make adjustments to the minutes.

3. Follow the same procedure to set the seconds indicator. Click on the area where seconds are displayed, and then use the up or down arrows to change the seconds.

4. For AM and PM, just click on one or the other and use the up or down arrow to switch between the two.

When you're done making the date and time changes, click on the "OK" button.

At the bottom of the clock and calendar windows are three buttons: "OK," "Cancel," and "Apply."

You will see these buttons many times in Windows so you should get to know what they mean.

• "OK" tells the computer that any changes made are correct and that it should make those changes and close the window.

• "Cancel" tells the computer not to make any changes and to close the window. If you think you may have made a wrong setting, or if you feel totally lost, just hit "Cancel." The result will be as though you never did anything at all.

• "Apply" tells the computer to use the changes you made. It's similar to clicking on the "OK" button, except that the window remains open. You could use this option if, for example, you just changed the time and want the computer to make that change before you begin setting the date.

B. Moving the task bar

You can move the task bar to any side of the desktop you want. When you first get your computer, Windows puts the task bar at the bottom of the screen. It's very simple to move the task bar in the following way.

Moving the Taskbar in Windows XP

1.   Make sure that all windows are closed and no programs are running.

2.   Move your pointer over the taskbar, placing it in any empty area. You can simply put the pointer in the middle of the taskbar. Just make sure you don't put the pointer over the clock or the "Start" button.

3.   Right click on an empty area of the task bar and make sure that there is not a check mark next to the "Lock the Taskbar" option. If there is a checkmark then select and click on the option to remove the checkmark. If there isn't a checkmark then left click on an empty area of the taskbar to close the menu.

4.   Click the left button, hold it down, and drag the taskbar to the top, bottom, right or left side of the screen.

5.   Release the mouse button.

All other versions of Windows

1. Make sure that all windows are closed and no programs are running.

2. Move your pointer over the task bar, placing it in any empty area. You can simply put the pointer in the middle of the task bar. Just make sure you don't put the pointer over the clock or the "Start" button.

3. Click the left button, hold it down, and drag the task bar to the top, bottom, right or left side of the screen.

4. Release the mouse button.

You can always move the task bar back if you put it in the wrong place.

III.
Windows XP

The following section explains how Windows XP differs from other Windows operating systems. It assumes that you've read the basic section of this book and that you understand fundamental computer skills and terms such as window, close gadget, and icon. If you don't understand what those things are, go back and read the beginning of this book, where all the basics are explained. If you have Windows XP or if you're just curious, read on.

A. Windows XP history

With the release of Windows XP, Microsoft has taken a large step toward a better computer operating system. Windows XP is much more than just an upgrade. It's a completely new and better operating system.

Windows XP, which stands for Windows Experience, is based on Windows NT. Because of that it has many benefits that make it one of the best operating systems for home computer use. For one thing, it's a lot more stable; you'll find that it will crash far less frequently. For example, if you're running several different programs on your computer at once and one of them crashes, you can simply close that program and continue on with the other programs that are currently running. Previously, a crash like the one described above might take the whole computer down with it. You'd lose all your work and have to restart your computer.

If you've ever experienced a crash with an earlier version of Windows, such as Windows 95, Windows 98 or Windows Me, you're familiar with the blue scan disk screen that greeted you after you turned on your computer following a crash. It scolded you for shutting down your computer improperly, and then it proceeded to scan your hard disk for errors. That took a few minutes—or longer.

Happily, all that is gone with Windows XP. At the center of Windows XP beats the heart of Windows NT. That combination provides a new and improved way to handle your files and hard disks called NT File System, or simply NTFS. NTFS keeps track of the state of your hard disk. Thus, if your system crashes or if the power goes out, NTFS won't require a disk scan when your computer starts up again.

Windows XP is also geared toward multiple users. If you share one computer among a few people, they can each be given their own account. Therefore you can have your own files and settings while your friends have their own. This gives individual users the capability to customize the computer according to their own needs and preferences.

B. Should you upgrade to Windows XP?

Windows XP is not for everyone. It requires a bit more computer horsepower than the other windows operating systems. Not everyone may wish to buy a new computer, so you need to carefully weigh the pros and the cons of upgrading to Windows XP.

If you're buying a new computer, the decision is simple. You should by all means purchase a computer that has Windows XP installed on it. With a new computer you can rest assured that it'll have enough computing power to run the new Windows.

On the other hand, if you're happy with your present computer but are still thinking of upgrading to Windows XP, you need to determine if your computer is powerful enough to run the new Windows.

KEEP IN MIND: The minimum system requirement for Windows XP is a computer running a 233 megahertz processor (CPU) with 64 megabytes of ram (Memory).

However, if your computer just meets Microsoft's minimum requirements, you're likely to be disappointed with its performance. Plan on 1) upgrading your present computer, or 2) buying a new one that more closely matches or exceeds the recommended system requirements.

Whichever route you take, you'll also need a Super VGA or better video card and about 1.5 Gigabytes of hard disk space.

If you can afford a new computer, then ideally you should have a Pentium 4 processor running at about 1 Gigahertz or more and 256 Mega Bytes of ram.

Don't forget about the hard drive. Although you can get by using a smaller 20 Gigabytes hard drive you'll be happier with a larger hard drive with about 40 Gigabytes of space — more if you can afford it.

If you can't or don't want to upgrade, then by all means continue to run Windows 98 or Windows Me on your computer. Both are still good operating systems, and you can probably get a few more years of service from them before you really need to upgrade.

C. The Windows XP desktop

At first glance the new Windows XP looks pretty much the same as the old Windows. From the user's point of view, the basic parts of Windows XP are the same as all the Windows before it. All the important changes have been made under the hood, so to speak.

For example, you'll still double click on icons on your desktop to open a program, and when you're done with a program you can still close the window by clicking on the close gadget in the upper right hand corner of the window. Windows XP may look a bit different to you, but that's mainly because Microsoft has given Windows XP a fresh look by changing the colors and shapes of things slightly.

If you're familiar with an older version of Windows, such as Window 95, Windows 98 or Windows Me, you should be able to get around in Windows XP fairly easily. The only frustration you may have with Windows XP is in finding some of the control panels or changing options, since Microsoft has moved a few locations of certain items.

The default Windows XP desktop

The biggest visible change made in Windows XP is in the Start menu and the taskbar. If the Start menu was important in using previous versions of Windows, it's absolutely imperative now. In fact, the default startup setting for a new Windows XP machine places *only* the Recycle Bin on the desktop and nothing else. This forces you to use the Start Menu to do just about anything with your computer.

If you don't like the new look of Windows XP, you can customize it to make it look and act more like previous versions of Windows. You'll learn how to customize Windows XP in the following section. For now, let's look at the new Start menu to understand why

Microsoft decided to make such a radical departure from previous versions of Windows.

One of the reasons that the default Windows XP desktop is so naked is that it gives users the ability to customize it, to make it look exactly the way they want it to look. For the first time, Windows users are given a clean slate for a desktop. There they can place any information they need in whatever manner they wish. Gone are the familiar desktop icons such as "My Computer," "Internet Explorer" and "My Documents."

Click on the 'Start' button and the Start menu appears. Observe that all the missing icons from previous versions of Windows have been collected and placed upon this menu. If you take a closer look, you'll notice that to help with organization, the Start menu is divided into several different parts.

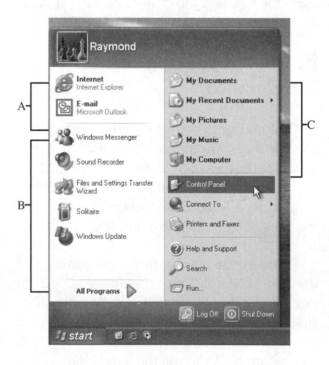

Start Menu Organization

A — Pinned Programs
B — Frequently Used Programs
C — "My" Section

One of the new features of Windows XP is that multiple users can use the same computer and customize it with their own preferences — without at all changing the settings of other users. To keep track of the different settings for different users, each user has an account. An account is usually a name or handle that identifies each individual user. At the very top of the Start menu is the name of the user or account that is currently logged on, along with a small picture that helps identify the account. If you're still unsure what a user account is, we'll go over that in more detail in the User Accounts section elsewhere in this book.

Directly below the user name, along the left side of the Start menu, is the section for shortcuts to frequently used programs. By default this section usually has "Internet" and "E-mail" options, but you can place or "pin" programs that you use frequently to this section of the Start menu. Think of it as a bulletin board on which you can pin programs.

D. Contextual menus

In order to learn how to pin a program to the Start Menu you need to understand some things about contextual menus. These are special menus that appear on the screen when you right click an icon on your desktop. They are called contextual because they change depending on the type of icon you use them with. Right clicking on different shortcuts will give you different menu selections.

Not all icons can be pinned to the Start menu. Only programs like word processors, games, utilities, etc., can be pinned to the Start menu. If you right click on an icon and the contextual menu that appears does not have the option, "Pin to Start menu," then it isn't possible to pin that type of item to the Start menu.

For example, say you use the built-in mini word processor called WordPad frequently.

Normally in order to start WordPad you would do the following:

1. Click on the Start button.

2. Click on "All Programs."

3. Click on "Accessories."

4. Click on "WordPad."

Please note that you may not have to click in steps 2 and 3. Many times simply putting the pointer over these items and holding it there (hovering) for a short period will open the next screen. I say "click" just so you'll make sure the option opens.

That's a lot of work just to open a program that you use daily. Before Windows XP appeared, you could create a shortcut to the WordPad program on your desktop by right clicking, dragging WordPad to your desktop, and then selecting "Create Shortcut here" from the menu that appeared. You can still do this with Windows XP, and there's nothing wrong with doing so. But if you're like most people, your desktop tends to become cluttered with all kinds of shortcuts. Before long, it becomes difficult to find the shortcut you want amid the jungle of shortcuts and other items on your desktop.

Windows XP offers a more elegant way to make the WordPad program easily accessible rather than making it just another item on a cluttered desktop. Simply pin WordPad to your Start menu and it's only one click away all the time.

To pin something to the Start menu, just right click on it and then select the "Pin to Start menu" option from the contextual menu. So the steps to pin WordPad to your Start menu are as follows.

1. Click on Start.

2. Click on "All Programs."

3. Click on "Accessories."

4. Right Click on "WordPad."

5. Click on the "Pin to Start menu" option of the contextual menu.

After doing this you should see WordPad in the upper left side of your Start menu, under "Internet" and "E-mail," the next time you click on the Start button. Keep in mind that, depending on how your computer was set up, you may have other items pinned to your Start menu as well.

The time may come when you no longer use WordPad and no longer need it on your Start menu. You can unpin it just as easily as you pinned it. Simply find the item you want to unpin in your Start menu and right click on it. Then choose the "Unpin from Start menu" option in the contextual menu. Immediately the pinned item will disappear. However, it isn't deleted or removed from your computer. It's only removed from the list on your Start menu. You'll still be able to find and run WordPad or any other program that you remove from the pinned area of the Start menu, just as you did before you pinned it there.

E. Most-used programs

The next section of the Start menu, right under the pinned programs section, is an area containing a list of programs that have been used recently. By default this area holds the six most used programs, but you can change that number from as few as none to as many as thirty.

The items on the list aren't simply the last few programs you've used. Windows keeps track of how often you use certain programs and puts the most-used programs in this list. It's sort of like a handy custom pinned program area that changes as you use your computer.

If you'd like to change the number of programs listed in this area, or if you simply want to clear the list so that it starts from a clean slate, follow these steps.

1. Right click on the Start button.

2. Choose "Properties" from the menu that appears.

3. From the Start menu tab click on the "Customize" button. (Note that this feature will not work if the "Classic Start Menu" option is selected.)

4. In the section entitled "Programs," change the number of items to be displayed by either typing in a new number or clicking on the up or down arrows next to the number. If you want to clear the list, click on the "Clear List" button.

5. Click on the "OK" buttons to close the properties windows.

F. All programs

The All Programs option is the area of the Start menu that enables you to find all the other programs that are installed on your computer but aren't displayed in any of the other areas of the Start menu.

Simply hovering over "All Programs" with your mouse pointer or clicking on it will open another window that displays the programs that are on your computer. Some of the options may have submenus that you can point to and open other lists. This option is just like the 'Programs' option of the Start menu in older versions of Windows.

"All Programs" is the first place you should look when you're trying to find a new program that you recently installed on your computer. It's also where you can find the basic built-in programs that come with Windows, such as WordPad, Calculator and Games.

G. "My" section of the start menu

The 'My' section of the Start menu is at the top of the second column on that menu. You can easily identify this section because all listed items start with "My." Depending on how your computer has been configured, some or all of the following items may be listed here: "My Documents," "My Recent Documents," "My Pictures," "My Music," "My Network Places" and "My Computer." If some of the items are missing when you first begin working with Windows XP on your computer, don't worry. You'll learn later how to customize the list so that all, none, or only selected items appear.

These items are used to organize the files and documents that you place into your computer. When you click on one of these links a new window opens to show the contents within each category. Of course, you still need to put the files and documents into these folders. That's not done automatically. For example, if you're working on a word processing document it's still up to you to make sure that you save it in the "My Documents" folder. Many times Windows will help you by suggesting a place to put the file or document. But you still have the freedom to save it anywhere else. It's a good idea to use these folders. Make this a habit. You'll find that it's a big help in keeping track of the files on your computer. Also, you'll have a place to start when you need to find something.

The only two exceptions to this rule are "My Recent Documents" and "My Computer," both of which differ from the others. "My Recent Documents" is a list of files that you have used lately. It holds only a few items, and as you open new files or use more programs this list will change. You can't place things into this folder. It's just a place to look for something you've used lately but whose file name you can't recall. How you use your computer determines how helpful "My Recent Documents" will be for you.

The "My Computer" item is similar to the 'My Computer' icon found on previous versions of Windows. If you click on it a window opens up that lets you gain access to the hard disks installed on your system and to any floppy disk, CD-ROM, or other item connected to your computer. In Windows XP, however, "My Computer" becomes an even more powerful tool when you right click on it and select the "Manage" option from the menu that appears.

Doing so opens up a new console that lets you perform a variety of management tasks. This management console is so new and powerful that an entire section has been devoted to it. For more information, see the "Management Console" section later in this book.

Below the "My" section of the Start menu is a group of items that let you control and configure parts of your computer. These items are called "Control Panel," "Connect To," and "Printers and Faxes."

The last two are pretty self explanatory. "Connect To" lets you connect to the Internet or other computers that you may have connected to your computer via a modem or small computer network.

"Printers and Faxes" lets you configure and use any Printers or Faxes that are connected to your computer. You can also add new printers and faxes to your system by clicking on this item after you've connected the printer or fax to your computer.

H. Control panel

The "Control Panel" is the main place you'll go to configure settings and to adjust how things look and act on your computer. You'll also use the control panel to add or remove programs or to perform maintenance on your system.

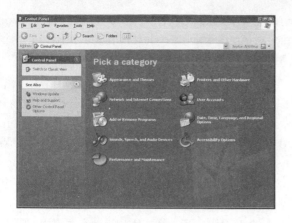

The control panel

In the Windows XP control panel, management options are grouped together by categories. There are nine different categories, and each one leads to other options and tools when you click on them.

If you're interested in changing the way Windows looks, click on the "Appearance and Themes" option. This opens a window containing tools to customize your desktop with a new photo or colored background. You can also choose a screen saver, customize the Start menu and task bar, or change the way folders look when you open them.

The "Network and Internet Connections" option lets you set up your modem to dial out to the Internet. Or, if you have a small computer network installed, you can use these controls to set up and configure your computer for use on the local network.

Other options in this window will let you edit or change your Internet connection or local network settings.

Clicking on "Add or Remove Programs" opens a window that lets you safely remove programs that you've installed on your computer. This is the only recommended way to remove a program once you've installed it on your computer.

This procedure does not include *files* that you may have created with programs. For example, if you use Microsoft Word to create a letter, you wouldn't use "Add or

Remove Programs" to remove the letter you created. Instead, you'd simply drag the letter into the recycle bin to get rid of it.

But if you were tired of using Microsoft Word and wanted to switch to a new or different word processor, you should remove Word from your computer with the "Add or Remove Programs" option in the control panel.

If you try to remove Word simply by dragging its folder into the recycle bin, you won't get rid of it completely. What's more, you'll risk making your computer unstable.

If you go to the "Add or Remove Programs" section and you don't see the program you want to remove in the list, then you can try dragging the program to the "Recycle Bin" to get rid of it. But always check "Add or Remove Programs" first to make sure it's not listed.

You can also use this section to add different parts of Windows that may not have been installed when Windows was initially installed on your computer. Click on the "Add/Remove Windows Components" button along the left side of the window and you'll be given the option to add or remove parts of windows from your computer.

Unless you have a compelling reason to do so, it's not a good idea to just want only remove or add parts of Windows. Unless you're instructed to do so, it's best to leave a working system alone. It's safe to look around if you're curious. Just remember always to click on the "Cancel" button to ensure that you don't make any changes that could harm your computer.

Three other options in the control panel are used to change and customize settings on your computer. They're self-explanatory options and you can play around with them if you're curious. If you just look at them, make sure that you always click on the "Cancel" button so you don't make any changes in Windows. The three options are "Printers and Other Hardware," "Sounds, Speech, and Audio Devices," "Date, Time, Language, and Regional Options."

Accessibility Options let you configure your computer for special needs. With these options you can change colors, choose a high contrast setting for poor eyesight, or even make the text on the screen larger.

One new option in the control panel is "User Accounts." With this you can create accounts that other people use when they are at your computer. This is of enormous help for families that need to share a computer among several people. By using different accounts for each person, you can control the files that each user sees as well as their individual options such as desktop picture and favorite websites.

There are two types of accounts: administrator and limited. It's a good idea to have only a few administrators and to make the other people limited accounts. As an administrator you can always change a person's account type if that becomes necessary.

If you are the only person who uses your computer, then there really isn't much need to use this option. Still, feel free to play around with it if you like. For more information about user accounts see the **Log Off option** section a little later on.

The final option in the control panel is the "Performance and Maintenance" section. This is a collection of tools that you can use to adjust your computer and make it run smoother and/or faster.

Unless you're an advanced user, you'll probably use only a few of these options. The most useful items are covered here. But as you learn more and become more confident with your computer, you can play around with some of the other options to see what they do.

I. Free up space on your hard disk

This option lets you clean up your hard disk by removing temporary files that accumulate on your computer as you use it. One of the options in this list is to empty the files into the recycle bin. If you've recently thrown away something and you think you may want to pull it back out of the recycle bin later on, uncheck this option. Once the files in the recycle bin are deleted, you can't retrieve them.

That's true of all the files that you remove with this option, but you needn't panic. The files that the computer removes by default are completely safe to get rid of. They are temporary files that get put on your computer as you browse the Internet, download programs, read email and install software. Getting rid of these files will not hurt the programs you use on your computer.

It's a good idea to use the hard disk clean up utility at least once a month just to make sure your collection of useless files doesn't get out of hand.

J. Rearrange items to make programs run faster

This is basically the disk defragmentation utility that was used in other versions of Windows. By using this utility all the programs, files and data stored on your computer's hard disk are moved around so that they're neatly place in order. Doing this may give your computer a small performance boost—which means it may run a tad faster.

If you're wondering how programs and files can get out of order on a hard disk, you need to understand how a hard disk operates. Since your computer is using the hard disk all the time, the data that's on it is constantly changing. When you create a new file or put something on your computer, it may get broken up into smaller parts that spread out over the hard disk. When you go to use the file or program again, the computer assembles all the little parts back together for you.

By defragmenting your hard disk, you're taking all the little parts and placing them closer to each other. Consequently, the computer doesn't need to look all over the hard disk in order to put the file back together for you. Since it now takes less time to retrieve a file, the computer will seem to run faster.

Don't expect a huge leap in speed by using this utility. Unless your hard disk is very, very fragmented, you probably won't notice much if any change in the speed of your system.

It's still a good idea to run this utility about once a month so the files on your computer don't get completely out of hand. Defragmenting can take a very long time — a day or even longer—if you wait until your hard disk is in dire need of organization. The amount of time depends on the size of your hard disk and the number of files on it.

I like to start this utility at night when I'm finished using the computer. That way it can run all night if it needs to, and I can check on it in the morning. If you don't like leaving your computer on all night, start the process before dinner or on a day that you watch television. Then check on the computer's progress every now and then.

If you perform this maintenance regularly, it won't take as long. I've seen hard drives that haven't been cleaned up in over a year. In such extreme cases it can take more than a day to finish the task. Keep in mind that you can't use the computer while it's defragmenting your hard disk. That's a long time for some of us to be without a computer!

K. Back up your data

This option helps you collect information about which files and programs are important to you. Then it helps you make backup copies of them for use in case your computer crashes and loses the information.

Note: Window XP Home edition users

If you're using Windows XP Home edition, you'll need to install the backup utility separately. Follow these steps.

1. Put your Windows XP Home CD into your computer.

2. If a blue installation window opens on your computer click the "Exit" button.

3. Click on "Start."

4. Click on "My Computer."

5. Double click on the CD-ROM drive that has the Windows XP Home CD.

6. Double click on the "Value Add" folder, then double click on the "MSFT" folder, and finally double click on the "NT Backup" folder.

7. Double click on the "Ntbackup" icon in the folder to start the installation.

If you can't find the file try searching for it as described in the next section.

If you're going to make large backups consisting of hundreds of programs and/or files, it's not a good idea to use 3.5 inch floppy disks. They don't hold enough information, and you could need hundreds of disks to make the backup. A better solution is to use something like a Zip disk, which holds greater amounts of information and can be removed from your computer.

One of the best methods for backing up is a tape drive. These are special machines that use magnetic tape similar to cassette tapes. Tape drives hold tons of information in a small package and are ideally suited for large back up purposes. Unfortunately, most home computers don't have tape backup because it's a bit pricey and is mostly used in business or the professions.

You should back up only the information that you absolutely need. Thus it's a good idea to pick and choose what you really need. If you have a program on CD-ROM or if it came with your computer and you have it on system disks that came packaged with your computer, you don't need to back it up. The CD-Rom or system disks are perfectly good backups of what you have on your computer.

What you really need to back up are the things you create on your computer — such as photographs from your digital camera or letters that you generate. One day you may need to retrieve such files, and to do so you need the program you used to create and save them. If for some reason you no longer have that program on your computer, you can use the program's CD-ROM that came with your computer as your backup. Once you've reloaded the program, just retrieve the photograph, letter, or whatever.

By following this advice you'll keep the number of things you back up to a minimum and you'll have the important materials when you need them. You'll also spend less time creating backups.

To make a backup just follow the steps in the wizard that walk you through the process. It's a good idea to know what you need to back up and where it is on your computer before you start this process. Otherwise you'll find yourself frantically searching for things and perhaps missing something.

One strategy I use is to store all the important material in designated folders on my computer. I use the "My Documents" folder for all the word processing files, and I have similar folders specifically designated to hold one kind of file. That way I can back up two or three folders with the confidence that I haven't overlooked any stray files.

Once you have a backup, the next logical question is what to do with it. That depends. The best way to use a backup is to keep it off site. That means you shouldn't keep it near your computer. In fact, it's a good habit to put backup materials in another building or even in a safe deposit box. Such security measures are common practice for preserving valuable papers such as birth or marriage certificates. They are no less valuable for preserving important and perhaps irreplaceable files created on your computer.

You may not think such precautions are necessary for you. That's fine, because only you can determine how important the safety of your backup is.

Another key to making a backup work is to do it regularly. You don't need to do it every day, but if you have important material on your computer, get in the habit of backing it up at least once a week. Again, you'll have to judge how often you need to back up, if at all.

L. Search and help

The next section on the Start menu is Search and Help. This is where you go when you have questions or need to find something on your computer, but you can't remember where it is or what it was called.

When you click on "Help and Support," the Help and Support window opens. Use your mouse to click on various topics that can help you answer basic questions you may have about using your computer or troubleshooting problems. Don't expect to find very specific or detailed help for every type of problem. This is primarily a general help section. If you connect to the Internet before you click on "Help and Support," you'll find more current topics and more detailed help.

The Help and Support window

The "Search" option is handy for those times when you can't find a file or program on your computer. When you click on it a new search window opens with several options for fine tuning your search.

The Search window

When the search window opens it's blank with some options on the left-hand column. Use the mouse to select the type of file that you're looking for, such as pictures, music, or documents. If you aren't sure what type of file you're looking for, then select the 'All files and folders' option and type part of the name or some other information into the appropriate fields that appear on the left hand column. When you're ready, click on the "Search" button.

Depending on the size of your computer's hard drive and the type of file you're looking for, a search can take quite a long time. When the search is finished a list of results will appear in the main part of the window on the right side.

If you don't find what you're looking for in the first attempt, try using some different options. Click on "More advanced options" to see if anything there looks like it might help you find your file.

If you still can't find the file, it may have been deleted or removed from your computer. If so, you'll probably not be able to locate or recover it. Once a file has been deleted it's very difficult to get it back unless you use special software. Even then it may be impossible to retrieve the file.

You'll notice that there are column names in the list of matches. The first column is called "Name" and it gives the exact name of each file in the list. The next column is called "In Folder," and it shows you where the file is located—in this case on the hard disk.

Now you'll learn how to find that file on the hard disk from the information given in the "In Folder" column. The information that leads you to your file's location is called a path. Just as you'd walk down a path to go some place, you follow the path given in the "In Folder" column to reach your file.

Let's say you found a file and it was in the folder labeled C:\Program Files\Microsoft. How would you go about opening the window on your computer containing that file?

Before you read the answer, think about this a bit. Take a good, long look at the path.

M. C:\Program Files\Microsoft

It might look a bit confusing at first, but take another look at it. Don't some of the parts look a little familiar? You should at least recognize the C: part of the path.

It's your hard disk. How do you get to your hard disk? Maybe you remember. Double click on "My Computer" and then double click on the C: drive.

Now you're moving. Take a close look at everything you see in the open C: drive window. You should find a folder called "Program Files." Now you decide to take a chance and double click on the folder called "Program Files." A new window opens up.

Take a look at everything in the new window. Sure enough, you'll find a folder called "Microsoft." By this time you should be feeling pretty confident. Next, double click on the "Microsoft" folder. A new window opens up with even more folders to browse through. So start looking at everything in this folder. Finally, you'll see a file named exactly like the file you found in the "Find" window. It's the file you've been looking for.

That was just an example. Your computer may or may not have the folders I used for the example, but the same logic would apply in searching for any file by using the "Find" window. The path is always given in a prescribed order. That way you can always find the file you're looking for.

Windows first gives you the drive letter where the file is located, followed by a backslash ("\"). Next, Windows tells you where to find the first folder, followed by another backslash, and then the next folder followed by yet another backslash. The series of identifying marks ends when you're at the exact folder containing the file you're looking for. Here's another way to look at this:

N. Drive letter:\Folder\Folder\Folder\...

If you remember this, you'll have cracked the code for all those complicated looking paths you see when you do a search. This is a very significant lesson that'll give you the power to find any file, anywhere, on

any drive on your computer. Please practice it whenever you can.

I'm always surprised by how many people I see using a computer every day who don't understand this one simple concept. Learn it. It'll serve you well, especially when you begin saving and loading files on your computer.

Let's say you searched for a file and the "In Folder" column reported that the file was located in "C:\Program Files\Microsoft\."

In shortened form, here's the step-by-step way to find that same folder used in the example:

1. Double click on the "My Computer" icon on the desktop.

2. Double click on the C: drive.

3. Double click on the "Program Files" folder.

4. Double click on the "Microsoft" folder. If you don't have a "Microsoft" folder, remember that this is just an example. Don't worry about it.

The "Microsoft" folder is now open in a window. You can scroll around, if necessary, to find the exact file you were looking for. Then you can move it, copy it, run it, or open it.

One tip you may find useful is to maximize the find window so that you can see more of the path. Sometimes the path is too long to fit within the "In Folder" column. You'll know this because the path will end in an ellipsis (...). This is Windows' way of letting you know that there is more information that you can't see.

If you see this and you need to know what the full path is, you can make the column wider so that you can see the full path. To do this, put the pointer at the top of the columns over the titles between the right edge of the "In Folder" column and the left edge of the next column. If you do this correctly, you will see the pointer change to a vertical bar with arrows pointing to the left and right. If you left click and then drag to the right, the "In Folder" column will get wider. Keep dragging until you can see the full path — then let go of the mouse button. Practice this for a bit. It will be handy to know how to do this at certain times.

You should also know that some paths and file names can look quite strange. Sometimes you will find a path or a file with a tilde (~) or and underline (_) in the name. This is normal.

Try one more example. If the file was reported to be in the C:\Windows\Temp\~E3064 folder, you'd find that folder by following the path described below.

1. Double click on the "My Computer" icon on the desktop.

2. Double click on the C: drive.

3. Double click on the "Windows" folder.

4. Double click on the "Temp" folder.

5. Double click on the "~E3064" folder.

Exercise #11

Practice looking for files and then finding them using the "My Computer" folder on the desktop. Can you do it without looking back in the lesson?

O. More advanced searches

Whenever you are looking for a file, you can specify a wild card in your search. For example, if you wanted to find all the files, programs and folders in your computer that started with the letter "J" you could type "J*" in the input box for the name of the file you are looking for. The "*" character tells Windows "everything". To the computer "J*" tells the computer to look for all files that start with the letter "J" and then everything else.

Previously we searched for all files that contained the word "set" in the "Named" input box. We could have typed in "*set*" and got the same results. What "*set*" tells the

computer is find all files, folders and programs that have any combination of letters and numbers, the word "set", and any other combination of letters. What the computer displayed was every single file name that had the word "set" anywhere in the name.

Let's take a look at some variations on this search. Say you wanted to find only the files that started with "set". How would you do that? Simply, just type "set*" and the computer will find all the files that start with set and then have anything else after that.

What about if you wanted to find files that ended in "set"? Think about this for moment. You want files that end in "set". You don't care what is before it so use the wildcard for the beginning and then you want "set". It would look like this: "*set".

What would happen if you just typed in "*" and did a search? You are asking the computer to find file names with anything in them. This search would give you a list of every single file, program and folder on your computer.

P. "Turn Off" / "Log Off"

The final part of the Start menu is at the very bottom and it usually has two options. "Log Off" and "Turn Off Computer." This is where you go when you've finished using your computer and want to turn it off or when you wish to let someone else use it.

The "Turn Off Computer" option does exactly what you would expect. When you click on it you are given a few options as to how you want to turn off your computer. The first option may be "Suspend" or "Hibernate." These options are really only used by people working with laptop or notebook computers. They allow you to put your computer into a low-power state to help preserve battery life. Then when you're ready you can turn your computer on and resume where you left off.

"Turn off" is the option to choose if you're finished using your computer and want to turn it off. After you click this option your computer will prepare for shutdown and then turn itself off. Some computers don't fully turn themselves off. If this is the case with yours, you'll see a screen that tells you it's safe to turn your computer off. Then you can manually turn your computer off by using the power button.

The "Restart" option is used when you want the computer to turn off and then start back up automatically. Usually you do this only after you've installed new software or when the computer starts to act oddly.

The other option on the Start menu is "Log Off," and it's new to most Windows users. To understand the reason for this option, remember that the new Windows XP makes it possible to share your computer with other people by creating an account for them. Additional users may customize their desktop and settings, thus creating their own personal computer.

Although this may seem strange, it's really a good idea. By using separate "user" accounts for each person who uses the computer, things can be kept in a much more organized fashion. There's nothing worse than letting someone use your computer for a few hours only to find that they've changed a setting or a preference that you like but they don't. Sometimes it's hard to find out what they did and how to get the computer back to the way it was.

With separate user accounts, individual users can change and customize the computer for themselves — without interfering with your personal settings. They can change the sounds, the picture on the desktop, the screen saver, and other things all without disturbing your own personal choices. Additional benefits of separate accounts include the capacity to achieve greater organization by keeping one user's files separate from another's. Files become easier to find. Also, if need be, files can be made secure so that User A won't be able to see what User B has been doing on the computer.

If you are the only person using your computer and there is only one account, then you'll never see the log on screen. But if you do share your computer with someone else, it's a good idea to create an account for each person who'll be using the computer. Then, after creating a second account, the next time you turn on your computer you'll be able to log onto your own account by clicking on it.

To set up or change the user accounts on your computer, you need to open the User Accounts control panel by following these steps.

1. Click on "Start."

2. Click on "Control Panel."

3. Click on "User Accounts."

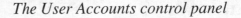

The User Accounts control panel

When you set up an account keep in mind that there are two types of accounts: computer administrator and limited user. As you would expect, the computer administrator account is the more powerful one. The computer administrator can change accounts, set passwords, and perform many other important functions. It's not a good idea to make everyone who uses your computer an administrator. If you did, the chances increase that, deliberately or accidentally, your computer could become a confusing tool to use. This would be another example of the old adage: "Too many cooks spoil the broth."

For this reason it's recommended that, as the administrator, you create limited user accounts for the other people who use your computer. You'll always have the ability, if needed, to change a limited user account into an administrator account.

Q. Managing your computer

If you right click on "My Computer" and choose the "Manage" option, a new window will open. This is the "Computer Management" console, which can be a useful way to manage and maintain your computer. Think of it as an advanced version of the "Control Panel."

The "Computer Management" window has some options that are both similar to and different options in the "Control Panel." If you're a computer novice or just getting your feet wet with Windows XP, use the "Control Panel" to create new users and to do other routine functions. As you become more comfortable with your computer knowledge, you can start to play around with the "Computer Management" window.

The "Computer Management" window is broken down into three main sections. The first is "System Tools." This is where you can see how your computer is running as well as view and configure some of the settings.

System Tools

The "Event Viewer" is where you can view a list of items that your computer has been working on lately. There are three types of logs kept by Windows. They are Application, Security and System. If you click on the little plus symbol next to the "Event Viewer," you'll be able to see the different logs that are kept there. Clicking on a log will display the events in it.

Unless you know what you're looking for, most of the items in this list will look

like Greek. But if you're having trouble with your computer, you may wish to check this area out to get some idea what may be causing the trouble.

The next section I'll point out is the "Local Users and Groups" item. This is similar to the 'User Accounts' option found in the "Control Panel." It's a bit more complex and will give you more options. This is really a section for the more experienced computer user, so don't bother trying to understand it until you've spent enough time playing with the "Control Panel" version of this tool.

The final item worth noting is the "Device Manager." This is where you go when you're having problems with that new mouse or network card, for example. If you just added some new hardware to your computer and it isn't functioning as it should, use the "Device Manger" to see what the problem is. You can even update or change the drivers for your hardware here.

Storage

The "Storage" section of the "Computer Management" window has a group of tools that will help you maintain the various disk drives and hard disk that may be attached to your computer.

The tool that you'll use most is the "Disk Defragmenter." Defragmenting your hard disk can help make your computer run smoother and faster. You don't need to do this all the time, but I recommend you do it every month or so. Be careful though, defragmenting a hard disk can take quite a long time. It's usually a good idea to make this the last thing you do before you go to bed and let the computer work over night. Defragmenting can take anywhere form a few minutes to as long as several hours.

To start the disk defragmenter click on the hard disk you want to defragment from the list at the top of the window, and then click the "Defragment" button. If you have only one hard disk, it'll automatically be selected for you.

Services and Applications

Services and Applications is the final section in the "Computer Management" window. Unless you're an advanced user, you won't get much out of this section. This is essentially a collection of tools that'll allow you to see all the different processes or services that are running on your computer at any given point in time.

Although your computer may look like it's doing nothing when you leave it alone, there are all kinds of little programs running in the background. Some of them are used to keep track of when to check for updates. Others are screen savers counting the idle seconds, waiting to begin. If for some reason you need to control these individual services, you can use this section to look at and change their settings.

R. Customizing Windows XP

Depending on how Windows XP was set up on your computer, it may look different from the pictures used in this book. The pictures are only for basic reference, and there's nothing wrong with your computer if it doesn't match the pictures in this book.

One of the easiest ways to customize Windows XP is to change the theme that Windows is using. A theme is a set of rules that tell Windows what colors to use as well as how some menus work and look.

To change the way various windows look, follow these steps.

1. Right click on the desktop.

2. Select Properties from the menu that appears and click on it with the left mouse button.

3. Click on the "Appearance" tab in the window that opens.

4. Click on the down-pointing arrow under the "Windows and buttons" section and choose either "Windows Classic style" or "Windows XP style."

5. Click on the 'OK' button and your new Windows XP will look more like the old Windows.

If you don't see the change, try opening up some windows and then going back and following the steps outlined above. Notice how the windows gadgets (in the upper right hand corner of the window) change. You should also notice that the "Start" button looks different.

If you click on the "Start" button you'll probably see that the menus that open up still look like the new Windows XP. You can change that too if you want to.

To change the way the "Start" menu works, do the following.

1. Right click on the "Start" menu.

2. Select Properties from the menu that appears and click on it with the left mouse button.

3. If it's not already selected, click on the "Start Menu" tab in the window that opens.

4. Near the bottom of the window you'll see two options. One is called "Start Menu" and the other is called "Classic Start Menu." Choose the one you want by clicking on the circle next to the option. When the circle has a black dot in the center of it, it means you've selected it.

5. Click on the "OK" button.

Keep in mind that the "Classic Start Menu" option is the one that looks and acts like the older version of Windows, whereas the "Start Menu" option is the one used by the new Windows XP version of the Start Menu.

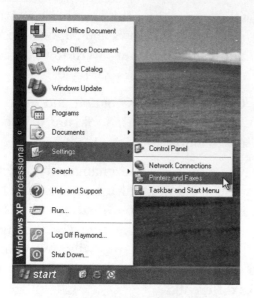

The Classic Start Menu

The default Windows XP Start Menu

Another way you can customize Windows XP is to select the icons that appear on your desktop. Depending on how your computer was set up, you may or may not have the "My Computer" and "My Documents" displayed on your desktop.

You can adjust and change what icons appear on your desktop with the following steps:

1. Right click on your desktop and select "Properties" from the menu that appears by clicking on it.

2. Click on the "Desktop" tab at the top of the "Display Properties" window that opened.

3. Near the bottom of the "Desktop" section is a button labeled "Customize Desktop." Click on it and the "Desktop Items" window will open.

4. In the "General" tab setting near the top you'll see some options for desktop icons. Check the ones you want displayed on your desktop by clicking on the box next to each type of icon. Then click on the "OK" button to close the "Desktop Items" window.

5. Click "OK" a second time to close the "Display Properties" window.

The new icons you choose to be displayed should be on your desktop. They usually appear in the upper left corner of the desktop.

Setting the desktop icons

IV.
Windows 95, 98, Me and 2000

If you have Windows XP please skip this topic and go ahead to Section V.

A. Using the start button

Move your pointer onto the "Start" button and left click. A list of options will appear. The important ones you should know about are the "Programs," "Settings," "Find," and "Shut Down" options. We'll cover these now.

B. Programs

To navigate through this list of options, just move the pointer onto the option you want to know more about.

If you want to see additional options, move the pointer over "Programs" and hold it there for a second or so. A new list of options then opens up, and you're able to see all the items under "Programs."

In this new list of options, notice that some of them look like yellow folders. Now move the pointer out over one of the items that looks like a folder. Hold the pointer there for a second. Still another new list of options will appear.

This is a lot like double clicking on the "My Computer" icon, then going into the C: drive, and then into the other folders. The difference is that the items listed under the "Start" button are programs already installed in your computer. So this is a quick way for you to find and run programs that you know have been installed.

Take some time to browse through the many programs that you find under the "Programs"

options. To run a program you find under the "Start" button, just move the pointer over the item. Then press the left mouse button once. The program will open automatically.

Try to find a program called "Solitaire," which is a game that comes with all versions of Windows. You can find it in Windows 98 by clicking on the "Start" button and then moving the pointer over the "Programs" option. Now move the pointer to the "Accessories" option, and then to the "Games" option. Finally, you'll see a list of games, and "Solitaire" will be one of them. Left click once on it and the game will run. Play with it for awhile. It's a great program for practicing your clicking and dragging skills.

Getting to Solitaire

C. Settings

"Settings" is the next option you should know about under the "Start" button. Put the pointer over the "Settings" option, and you'll see more options pop up. Take a close look at them. Two are called "Control Panel" and "Printers." Where have you seen these options before?

Put the pointer over the "Start" button again and click on it to make the list of options disappear. Now open up the "My Computer" folder on your desktop.

Among the list of drives and folders found in the "My Computer" folder, you'll notice that one folder is named "Control Panel" and another is named "Printers." Sure enough, these are the same folders you saw earlier.

You'll find that quite often. In Windows there are different ways to get to the same destination. As you become more proficient with Windows, you'll start to choose your own way of doing things. Just as you have a favorite system for shopping in a super-market, you'll have a favorite system for getting around in Windows.

Remember this when you're watching someone else use Windows. The way they do something may be different from the way you do it. It doesn't mean that they're right and you're wrong.

Now back to the "Start" button. Click on it and move the pointer back over the "Settings" option. Now left click on the "Control Panel" option and watch what happens. A new window opens, a special one that lets you adjust settings on Windows. Remember how to get to this window. You'll be gaining more experience with it later on. For now, just close the "Control Panel" window and go back to the "Start" button.

Find All Files Window

D. Find

The next option is "Find." Left click on "Start" and put your mouse pointer over "Find." In Windows 98 a list of options will appear. Move the pointer over the "Files or Folders" option and left click on it.

Once you left click on the "Find" option, the "Find" window opens up. This is a very handy program for those of us who occasion-ally have trouble remembering where we put something. "Find" helps you to locate something, and that can be quite handy.

"Find" will quickly search your computer for items that match the description you type in. Then you'll get a list of any items that could be a match for your lost file.

Take another look at the "Find" window. Notice that there are several input lines. An input line is a blank, white rectangle where you can type letters. Each input line is identified with a name, so you'll know what type of information to type. For instance, the input box called "Named" is asking you to input (type) the name of the file you're looking for. For this example, click on the "Named" input box and then type in the word "set."

There's another type of input box you can try, named "Look in." This is a white box with an arrow pointing down. Move the pointer over the down arrow and press the left mouse button once. A list drops down from the input box. Appropriately, it's called a drop down list, and you'll see these in many other windows.

The input box is telling you that only certain things can be selected here. When you click on the arrow, a list of choices drops down. You may also see a scroll bar at the right edge of the list. This means that you can scroll up or down, find the option in the list designated C:, and then left click to select it. When you do, the drop down list will disappear and the C: option will be showing in the input box, indicating that this is the option you selected. If you make a mistake and select the wrong item, just click on the arrow again. You'll be able to select another option from the drop down list.

There's one more setting on this window you should know about. It's the small white checkbox labelled "Include Subfolders." This is another type of input box. Click on the box to make a check mark appear or disappear. You'll want to have the check mark in the box so that the "Find" program will search in every single folder on the C: drive.

Now you're ready to start the search. Click on the "Find Now" button in this window. Windows will immediately start to go through the hard disk. As the "Find" program finds possible matches, they'll show up in the bottom part of the window. Notice how every possible program or file with the word "Set" in its name will show up. You could improve the search if you typed in a more specific name, but sometimes you just can't remember precisely what you called something.

In the list of possible matches, you'll see a scroll bar at the end of the window that lets you go through all the possible matches. You could maximize this window to allow more matches to fit into it.

You'll notice that there are column names in the list of matches. The first column is called "Name" and it gives the exact name of each file in the list. The next column is called "In Folder," and it shows you where the file is located — in this case on the hard disk.

Now you'll learn how to find that file on the hard disk from the information given in the "In Folder" column. The information that leads you to your file's location is called a path. Just as you'd walk down a path to go some place, you follow the path given in the "In Folder" column to reach your file.

Let's say you found a file and it was in the folder labeled C:\Program Files\Microsoft. How would you go about opening the window on your computer containing that file?

Before you read the answer, think about this a bit. Take a good, long look at the path.

E. C:\Program Files\Microsoft

It might look a bit confusing at first, but take another look at it. Don't some of the parts look a little familiar.? You should at least recognize the C: part of the path. It's your hard disk. How do you get to your hard disk? Maybe you remember. Double click on "My Computer" and then double click on the C: drive.

Now you're moving. Take a close look at everything you see in the open C: drive window. You should find a folder called "Program Files." Now you decide to take a chance and double click on the folder called "Program Files." A new window opens up.

Take a look at everything in the new window. Sure enough, you'll find a folder called "Microsoft." By this time you should be feeling pretty confident. Next, double click on the "Microsoft" folder. A new window opens up with even more folders to browse through. So start looking at everything in this folder. Finally, you'll see a file named exactly like the file you found in the "Find" window. It's the file you've been looking for.

That was just an example. Your computer may or may not have the folders I used for the example, but the same logic would apply in searching for any file by using the "Find" window. The path is always given in a prescribed order. That way you can always find the file you're looking for.

Windows first gives you the drive letter where the file is located, followed by a backslash ("\"). Next, Windows tells you where to find the first folder, followed by another backslash, and then the next folder followed by yet another backslash. The series of identifying marks ends when you're at the exact folder containing the file you're looking for. Here's another way to look at this:

F. Drive letter:\Folder\Folder\Folder\...

If you remember this, you'll have cracked the code for all those complicated looking paths you see when you do a search. This is a very significant lesson that'll give you the power to find any file, anywhere, on any drive on your computer. Please practice it whenever you can.

I'm always surprised by how many people I see using a computer every day who don't understand this one simple concept. Learn it. It'll serve you well, especially when you begin saving and loading files on your computer.

In shortened form, here's the step-by-step way to find that same folder used in the example:

1. Double click on the "My Computer" icon on the desktop.

2. Double click on the C: drive.

3. Double click on the "Program Files" folder.

4. Double click on the "Microsoft" folder. If you don't have a "Microsoft" folder, remember that this is just an example. Don't worry about it.

The "Microsoft" folder is now open in a window. You can scroll around, if necessary, to find the exact file you were looking for. Then you can move it, copy it, run it, or open it.

One tip you may find useful is to maximize the find window so that you can see more of the path. Sometimes the path is too long to fit within the "In Folder" column. You'll know this because the path will end in an ellipsis (...). This is Windows' way of letting you know that there is more information that you can't see.

If you see this and you need to know what the full path is, you can make the column wider so that you can see the full path. To do this, put the pointer at the top of the columns over the titles between the right edge of the "In Folder" column and the left edge of the next column. If you do this correctly, you will see the pointer change to a vertical bar with arrows pointing to the left and right. If you left click and then drag to the right, the "In Folder" column will get wider. Keep dragging until you can see the full path — then let go of the mouse button. Practice this for a bit. It will be handy to know how to do this at certain times.

You should also know that some paths and file names can look quite strange. Sometimes you will find a path or a file with a tilde (~) or and underline (_) in the name. This is normal.

Try one more example. If the file was reported to be in the C:\Windows\Temp\~E3064 folder, you'd find that folder by following the path described below.

1. Double click on the "My Computer" icon on the desktop.

2. Double click on the C: drive.

3. Double click on the "Windows" folder.

4. Double click on the "Temp" folder.

5. Double click on the "~E3064" folder.

Exercise #11

Practice looking for files and then finding them using the "My Computer" folder on the desktop. Can you do it without looking back in the lesson?

G. More advanced searches

Whenever you are looking for a file, you can specify a wild card in your search. For example, if you wanted to find all the files, programs and folders in your computer that started with the letter "J" you could type "J*" in the input box for the name of the file you are looking for. The "*" character tells Windows "everything". To the computer "J*" tells the computer to look for all files that start with the letter "J" and then everything else.

Previously we searched for all files that contained the word "set" in the "Named" input box. We could have typed in "*set*" and got the same results. What "*set*" tells the computer is find all files, folders and programs that have any combination of letters and numbers, the word "set", and any other combination of letters. What the computer displayed was every single file name that had the word "set" anywhere in the name.

Let's take a look at some variations on this search. Say you wanted to find only the files that started with "set". How would you do that? Simply, just type "set*" and the computer will find all the files that start with set and then have anything else after that.

What about if you wanted to find files that ended in "set"? Think about this for moment. You want files that end in "set". You don't care what is before it so use the wildcard for the beginning and then you want "set". It would look like this: "*set".

What would happen if you just typed in "*" and did a search? You are asking the computer to find file names with anything in them. This search would give you a list of every single file, program and folder on your computer.

H. Shutting down your computer

The last main option under the "Start" button is "Shut Down." Every time you want to turn you computer off, you must use this option. If you don't, if you just turn off the computer without first using the "Shut Down" option, you may lose information that's stored on your hard drive. To make sure this doesn't happen, follow the shut down procedure each time you turn the computer off.

When you select "Shut Down" from the pop up list, a new window opens with a list of options. Depending on what's loaded onto your computer, you may not have all of these options or you may have some more.

- Stand by

- Shut down

- Restart

- Restart in MS-DOS mode

If you're just going to leave your computer for a few hours, you can select the "Stand By" option. This puts your computer into a power-saving mode that uses less electricity and extends the life of your hard disks. As soon as you move the mouse or press any key on the keyboard, your computer will start back up exactly where you left off.

If you're turning your computer off for the day, choose "Shut Down." This option closes all the windows you may have open and then prepares the computer to shut off completely. When your machine is ready to be turned off, you'll see a message on the screen that reads "It's now safe to shut down your computer." No, the computer won't blow up if you shut it down before getting this message. But your files will be much safer if you wait for the message.

The newest computers will actually turn themselves off automatically. All you do is select the "Shut Down" option, press the "OK" button, and the computer will do the rest. On these machines you won't see the message telling you that it's safe to turn the computer off.

The "Restart" option is used when you've installed new software programs. For some of these programs to work properly, you need to restart the computer. This is just like turning the computer off and back on all in one step. Once you select this option and press the "OK" button, everything will proceed automatically.

You can also use the "Restart" option if you feel that your computer isn't acting properly. Even though they aren't human, computers can sometimes start acting goofy. They freeze up. Or they get very slow. Sometimes they just stop working. Various things can cause such "bad behavior."

As you become used to your computer, you'll be more aware of when it just doesn't seem to be working properly. Most of the time, you can simply restart it to return things to normal. Like a child, it needs to have an occasional "time out."

The last option is for "DOS," which refers to an old, outdated way of using your computer. Chances are you'll never need to use this option. In any case, if you get some software that requires "DOS," the instructions will explain what you need to do.

Remember. Each time you shut down your computer you'll lose work you're doing unless you saved it. So make sure you save work and close all programs and windows before you choose the option for shutting down.

If you're in the middle of something and get interrupted, use the "Stand By" option. That'll put the computer on pause. Later, you can come back to where you were working just by moving the mouse or pressing a few keys on the keyboard.

Exercise #12
Answer the following

When would you use the following options?

1. Shut Down _____

_____

2. Restart _____

_____

3. Stand By _____

_____

I. Windows settings

In this section you'll learn about features in Windows that allow you to customize it. You can make settings and adjustments to the way Windows looks and runs.

You should be familiar with all the concepts presented to you in this course before you start experimenting with any of these options. When you change the settings described below, your computer will look and act slightly different. Icons may not look the way they're described in this course. Parts of the desktop may be in other places or even hidden. If you don't have a good grasp of Windows, this can be confusing.

Go back and review previous sections if you feel you need to become more comfortable with any part of Windows.

J. Task bar options

In an earlier section you learned how to move the task bar around the screen. You can choose other options for the task bar.

If you want to enlarge the task bar, put the pointer right at the edge of the task bar where it meets the desktop. The pointer will change into a double-headed arrow. You can then drag and drop, pulling the task bar's long edge out and making it larger (thicker).

You can also do the opposite. If the task bar is in the way, again move the pointer over the area where the taskbar and the desktop meet. When the double-headed arrow appears, push in on the task bar to make it become much smaller (a thin line). Release the mouse button, and now the task bar will be as small as it can get. However, if you want to use the task bar, you'll have to grab it and pull it out again.

There are other things you can do with the task bar. Move the pointer over an empty part of it and press the right mouse button.

A box of listed options will appear. Now move the pointer over the word "Properties" and left click.

When you do this, a new window opens up. It should look like this ...

Task Bar Properties Window

You have what are called tabs at the top that let you choose between the "Taskbar Options" or the "Start Menu Programs." Many types of selection windows that deal with settings will display this tab format at the top. This helps to group similar settings.

To make sure that you're looking at the right set of options, move the pointer on top of the tab with the words "Taskbar Options" and left click.

This window is now showing you a list of four options for the task bar with check boxes next to them. The options are:

- Always on top
- Auto hide
- Show small icons in Start menu
- Show clock

"Always on top" should be checked. It makes sure that you'll always be able to get to the task bar. It keeps any other window from getting on top of it and blocking it from your view. If you don't have this checked when you open a window and maximize it, you won't be able to see the task bar. That can be frustrating when you need to get to the task bar.

"Auto hide" is a special feature that makes the taskbar fold up into a thin line when you're not using it. When you need to use the task bar, you just bump the pointer over the thin line and the task bar will unfold so you can see it. This is sometimes a handy setting, especially when you're using a program that needs more screen space.

"Show small icons in Start menu" reduces the size of the text and pictures that appear when you click on the "Start" button.

"Show clock" does exactly what it says. If you uncheck this option, thc clock will disappear from the taskbar.

Feel free to play with these options as you wish. You can always come back and change them whenever you need to. When you're done making changes, just click on the "OK" button at the bottom of the window.

K. Your control panel

Open the Control Panel.

1. Click on the "Start" button.

2. Click on "Settings."

3. Click on "Control Panel."

You're now looking under the hood of Windows. In this window you can make many changes to your computer. But there are some settings you probably shouldn't play with until you gain a better understanding of your machine.

In this section you'll learn about the following items in your "Control Panel."

- Add New Hardware
- Add/Remove Programs
- Desktop Themes
- Mouse
- Sounds

L. Adding new hardware

A complete explanation of the process of adding to or modifying your computer is well beyond the scope of this text. I can only point out where the option for adding new hardware exists in case you ever need to know where it is.

If you're going to install, say, a new video card or some other addition on your computer, use this icon to detect the new hardware (computer part) that you've added. Generally the instructions that come with any new part you're adding will guide you though the installation process.

M. Adding programs

You'll use this option often. Anytime you install new software onto your computer, it makes lots of changes to all kinds of settings in Windows. If you want to get rid of a program by just dragging it into the "Recycle Bin," you won't necessarily get rid of all the little parts of the program.

One of the major reasons so many new computer users have problems with their computers is that they've installed or removed software incorrectly.

If you just drag a program or folder containing a program into the "Recycle Bin," your computer may seem to act fine — until you turn it off and then start it back up later. At that point you may find that you're getting all kinds of errors or problems. Why is this so? Because Windows is still looking for the program you deleted. You see, you have to let Windows know when you take a program off your computer.

To make sure that a program gets taken off your computer properly, you'll need to use the "Add/Remove Programs" option. Double click on this icon. You'll see a window with three tabs at the top:

- Install/Uninstall
- Windows Setup
- Startup Disk

N. Installing a new program

This set of options can be reached by clicking on the words "Install/Uninstall" in the tabs across the top.

You'll see some instructions that say "To install a new program from a floppy disk or CD-ROM drive, click install."

You won't use this option very often. Most of the time when you buy a new program it'll automatically install when you put the CD into the drive. Otherwise, check the instructions that came with the new program. Always follow the manufacturer's installation instructions.

If those instructions don't tell you to use this icon in the "Control Panel," then don't. The company should know the best way to put its program on your computer. If all else fails, then come to this menu to install the software.

The bottom half of this window has the following message:

"Windows can automatically remove the following software. To remove a program or to modify its installed components, select it from the list and click Add/Remove."

You should always check to see if the program you want to remove from your computer is listed in this window. If it is, click on it to highlight it. Then click the "Add/Remove" button.

This will make sure that Windows knows that the program is removed and that it can try getting rid of all the little parts of the program.

If you don't see the program you're trying to remove from your computer in this list, then check the program's instructions to see if anything is said about how to remove the program.

When all else fails, you can try to drag the program and any folders associated with it into the "Recycle" bin. Then try using your computer for a day or two before you empty the "Recycle" bin — just to make sure you didn't remove (delete) anything that was needed for your computer to run properly.

O. Installing options

Move your pointer on top of the words "Windows Setup" and click once. A new group of settings will appear.

This is where you can add or remove little parts of Windows. For example, if your computer doesn't have the "Solitaire" game installed, you can add it here.

Just double click on a category name and a new list will open. Click on the white boxes next to the options you want to install. This puts check marks inside the boxes. Then click on "OK" and the new part will be installed into Windows.

If you double click on an option name and a new list doesn't open, this means that there are no other options at this location. Just click the white box next to it to select it.

For example, to add the "Solitaire" game, use the following steps.

1. Double click on the word "Accessories."

2. In the new list that opens find the "Games" option. Put a check mark in the white box by clicking on the white box.

3. Click the "OK" button. This will bring you back to the main options screen again. If you want to make more changes, you can at this time.

4. Click on the "OK" button and the changes will be loaded onto your computer.

You should have the Windows CD handy when you do this. Your computer may ask for it.

You can also do the opposite. If you wanted to remove the Solitaire game from your computer, just follow the above instructions, but remove the check mark from the white box next to the "Games" option.

P. Desktop themes

This option may not be installed on your computer. In Windows 95 you get it with the "Plus!" software package you can buy separately.

In Windows 98 the option can be installed by using the "Add/Remove Programs."

Selecting a desktop theme is kind of like having your room decorated. A theme is a collection of special wallpaper, screen saver, new icons and pointers. All are designed to be used together to create a special theme for your computer.

For example, if you were to choose a space theme, the wallpaper might be a solar system, the pointer a spaceship, and the icons for "My Computer" and "Recycle Bin" could be different planets.

There are all kinds of desktop themes. You can buy them or collect them from places on the Internet. Microsoft, for example, has some they give out on their web site.

When you double click on "Desktop Themes," a window opens that lets you pick a theme from a list of the ones that are currently on your computer. You can also adjust the different components of the theme by selecting the other options.

Desk Top Themes

Q. Using the mouse

In the control panel is an icon of a mouse that's logically called "Mouse."

If you double click on it you'll see options that you can use to customize the mouse and pointers on your computer.

The first set of options, "Buttons," lets you choose between right- or left-hand operation. If you select a left-handed mouse, the left and right mouse button functions will be reversed. So instead of a double left click to run a program, you'd use a double right click.

You can also choose the double click speed by using the slider in the bottom half of the screen. After choosing a double click speed, you can test it in the box to the right. Just double click, and if the jack-in-the-box jumps out or goes back into his box, you've double clicked.

If you set the slider all the way to slow, you can pause longer between clicks to complete a double click. Slide the setting all the way over to fast, and you may not be able to double click fast enough to make it work.

A tip: If you do happen to make the double click speed so fast you can't successfully double click, use the "Enter" key on the keyboard to get into your programs and to run the mouse configuration screen.

Just single left click to select the icon or program. When it's highlighted just hit the "Enter" key on your keyboard to make the program, file or folder open/run.

R. Sounds

If you double click on this option in the "Control Panel," you can choose what sounds Windows plays when certain things happen.

Your computer most likely plays music or sounds when you start or shut down as well as when Windows needs to draw your attention to a mistake you've made.

You can change all of these sounds by using this window. Just click on an "event" that you want a sound for. Then choose a desired sound from the list. You can choose other files by using the browse button. This will open a navigation window where you can look through your disks and find a sound file that you want Windows to use.

The play button lets you preview the sound by playing it for you. If you assemble a group of sounds that you like, you can save them as a scheme. Then you can later pick this scheme out of the list in the lower part of the window.

When you click on the "OK" button, the changes take effect.

Notice that you can change the sounds, wallpaper, pointers, and window colors from the "Desktop Themes" window. I recommend using this window to make any of those changes since you'll be able to work on everything all at once.

S. Taking care of windows

In this section you'll learn basic things you can do to help keep your computer running smoothly—much like changing the oil in your car. You don't have to do these things every day, but you should have a schedule and do them every so often.

You can do three basic things to help your computer work better.

1. Scan the hard disk for any errors.

2. De-fragment the hard drive so that the drive runs quicker and smoother.

3. Check available free space on your hard disk.

Close all programs or windows and double click on "My Computer." This is the window you'll use to perform routine maintenance on your computer.

Right click on the C: drive and choose properties from the menu list that pops up. The first screen you should see is the "General" settings.

In this screen is a pie chart showing the percentage of your hard disk that's being used for programs versus free space.

At the top of this window you'll see an input box that's titled "Label:". You can type in a name here that will show up in the "My Computer" window. This isn't necessary, but some people do like to have names for each of their drives.

If you look at the chart at the bottom of the screen, you can see how much free space remains on your hard disk. When the pie chart starts to show less than 20% free space, it may be time to start thinking about getting old files, folders and/or programs off the computer.

If there are old games or programs that you no longer use, get rid of them as just described under the topic "Adding Programs." If you simply can't afford to get rid of anything, you may want to buy another hard drive or get a bigger hard drive.

By the way, if anyone ever asks you how big your hard drive is, you can get the answer from this window. At the end of the information line titled "Capacity:" is a number ending in "GB," like "7.80GB." This is the size of your hard disk in gigabytes. Usually you round up or down to the nearest whole number, so the example above would be called an eight-gigabyte hard drive.

T. Scandisk

Now put the cursor over the "Tools" tab and left click on it. This will show you a group of options you'll use to check and maintain your drive(s).

You'll see three sections in this window.

The top section, "Error Checking," is an option used to check your disks for any errors that might be on them. You should use this feature about once a month or so.

Click on the "Check Now" button and the scandisk window will open. You can check the different disk drives that are attached to your computer. The ones you'll be checking most often are the internal hard drives on your system.

You should do a "Standard" check, but if your computer is acting strange you can try a "Thorough" test. The "Thorough" test takes much longer, so it's not advised that you use this every time. You could do the "Thorough" test two or three times a year.

You should also have a check mark next to "Automatically fix errors." Then click on the "Start" button and leave your computer alone while it docs thc tcst. Depending on the size of the hard disk, the test may take quite a bit of time.

U. Defragmentation

At the bottom of the "Tools" screen is the "Defragmentation status" section.

When you load programs or files onto your computer, they don't always get put on the same part of your drive. Sometimes they get scattered all over. When you go to run these programs, the computer has to look all over to find all the parts before it can run the program for you. This takes up time. It's like having all the ingredients for a cake scattered around your house. You'd have to go from room to room collecting them before you could start baking.

When you run the defragmentation program, it looks for scattered files and tries to bring them close together or all in the same place. That way, when you run or open these programs or files, they'll load more quickly.

You should do this after you get done scanning the drive for errors. I'd suggest about once every month.

Click on the "Check Now" button to have the computer start defragmenting your hard drive.

V.
Desktop Options

No matter what version of Windows you are using, continue reading here.

A. Desktop options

Other options you may find useful are found in the desktop properties. To get to these options, right click on an empty area of the desktop. Then left click on the "Properties" option in the pop up box.

The important tabs you should know about in Windows 95 are:

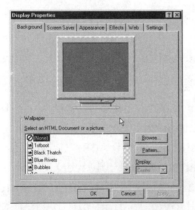

- Background
- Screen Saver
- Appearance
- Plus!
- Settings

These settings are basically the same as those in Windows 98, Windows 2000 and Windows XP. The "Plus!" setting may not be on your Windows 95 computer. "Plus!" is an additional piece of software that you have to buy separately for Windows 95.

If you do have "Plus!" it has the same set of options and settings as the "Effects" tab in Windows 98 and Windows 2000.

If you don't have this option in your Window 95, don't worry. You can probably still buy it if you really want to. It'll give you some extra screen savers and wallpaper pictures. But it's not necessary.

For descriptions of these options, see the Windows 98 and Windows 2000 sections that follow.

In Windows 98 and Windows 2000 the options you should know about across the top are:

- Background
- Screen Saver
- Appearance
- Effects
- Settings

B. Your screen background

Let's choose a "Wallpaper," which is simply a picture that can be displayed on your desktop. Windows has some wallpapers already installed, and you can have some fun seeing what they look like.

If you don't want a picture as your desktop, you can have a pattern. These are small graphics that fill your desktop. They are wallpaper that resembles drawings more than pictures.

C. Your screen saver

Click on this tab and you'll get choices as to what screen saver, if any, you'd like to have on your computer.

In the "Screen Saver" input box, click on the down arrow and a list of available screen savers will be displayed. Then you can set the time in minutes to determine how long it takes before the screen saver appears on the screen.

If you click on the "Settings" button, you'll see some other options for the screen saver. The options are different for each screen saver. But they all let you change such things as how fast the screen saver moves across the screen or what it types on the screen. Play with them and see what results you get.

There's a little check box that has "Password protected" next to it. If you check this box, your computer will ask you for a password whenever you want to stop the screen saver. If you're working in an office setting, this can be handy for keeping other people from seeing what you're using your computer for. If you forget your password, though, you too will be locked out of your own computer. So if you use this option, make sure you choose a password you won't forget.

To set the password, just click on the "Change" button. You can't click on this button until you first click in the box next to "Password protected." This puts a check mark in the box.

D. Appearance

With this tab you can change the way Windows looks. If you click on the down arrow next to the input box for "Scheme:" you'll see a list of installed Schemes. Click on a few of these and you'll see in the display some examples of what Windows will look like if you click on "OK" or "Apply."

You can also change individual items by using the drop down list in the "items" section of the page. For instance, you can choose the kind of font (what the text looks like) that will appear in the various windows, as well as the colors of various sections of the windows.

If you really want to give yourself a headache, try turning the lights down in your room and selecting "High Contrast White" from the "Scheme" list.

E. Effects

In this section you can change the way icons look. You could change the icon for "My Computer" by clicking once on the icon in the display to highlight it and then clicking on the "Change Icon" button. You'll then see a group of available icons, any of which you can substitute for the "My Computer" icon.

If you try out some icons but decide you'd really like to go back to the original icons, no problem. Just change them as you did earlier. Or simply click on the "Default Icon" button and Windows will make the icon picture look the way it used to.

There are some check boxes in this window too. You can play with these if you want — they're fairly self-explanatory. If you're not sure what they do, try one and see if you notice any difference in your desktop. You'll have to click the "OK" button before any change will occur. This can give you something to do on a rainy day.

F. Settings

Perhaps the most useful part of the desktop properties is the "Settings" tab. This is where you can learn how many colors your computer will use to make the pictures you see, as well as how to determine the resolution of the screen.

Resolution refers to the number of dots there are across your screen. If you get real close to your computer and — using a magnifying glass if you need to — look at the screen, you'll notice that it's really just a bunch of dots. The dots are called pixels.

If you looked at your TV screen very closely, you'd see that it too is made up of dots. However, your computer monitor has much smaller dots and many more of them. That's what gives it a sharper picture. So the more dots you have the better your graphics will look, for the most part.

Take out some graph paper and try to draw a circle using a 6 squares by 6 squares portion of the graph paper. Now try it using 20 squares by 20 squares. Clearly, the more squares (dots) you use, the smoother the curve you're able to make, and the better the circle you're able to draw. You should now understand why the number of dots determines how well your computer can draw things. This concept is called screen resolution.

Depending on what type of graphic card you have installed in your computer, you'll be able to get many different screen resolutions. Standard resolution is 640 X 480 pixels. That means if you were to count each dot across your screen there would be 640 of them, and if you counted each dot running down your computer there would be 480 of them.

If you increase this one notch to 800 X 600 pixels, you'll have many more dots on the screen and objects will appear smoother. You'll also have a larger desktop. That's because if an icon is, say, 100 pixels by 100 pixels in one screen resolution, it'll still be the same 100 pixels by 100 pixels in a higher or lower resolution.

But when you select a higher resolution, the dots have to be squeezed closer together. This makes the icon appear smaller. You can play with these settings if you want to. Remember, if you don't like them you can change them back.

The other option in this window is "Colors."

Depending on the type of video card you have in your computer, you'll have different options. Generally, the more colors, the better and the more lifelike pictures will look on your screen. Watch out, though. The more colors you choose the more demands you'll be making on the computer to draw all of them. If your computer starts to slow down too much, just back off on the colors a bit.

Some of the choices in color you have are:

• 16 color
• 256 color
• High Color (16 bit)
• True Color (24 bit)
• True Color (32 bit)

You may not have some of these or you may have more, depending on your video card. If you really want to see the impact of colors on the way things look on your computer choose "16 Color" and click on "OK."

Sometimes Windows will warn you to test the settings first. Just click "OK" and let Windows do the testing it wants to. Also, sometimes you may have to restart your computer to change the colors. Windows will alert you if this is needed. Just click on "Yes" or "No" and the rest is automatic.

"16 color" means that your machine will use only 16 colors to draw everything on the screen. It looks truly bad, as you may have already seen. But try it if you want.

Most of the time, you shouldn't use any fewer than 256 colors. This is the minimum amount of colors needed to make basic, acceptable pictures.

If your computer can display it, use "True Color (24 bit)." This gives the computer millions of colors to use, and your photographs will look like they do in real life.

If your computer can't handle many colors, just back down on the colors until you reach a happy medium. There's nothing more frustrating than waiting for your computer to catch up to you.

VI.
Files ... Loading Them & Saving Them

By this time you should have a basic working knowledge of how to use Windows. You can select something, open it, and then resize the window any way you want. You also know how to minimize and close a window.

You should also be quite comfortable using the mouse. If you aren't, go back and review the previous sections. This is important, because from now on I'll be assuming that you know what it means to close a window, double click, and scroll.

Remember that a file is a collection of information.

Some files contain the information to run a program. These are called "Programs." Some files contain information on how a program is to be set up. These are called "Settings Files." Other files contain information to be used with a program. These are referred to as just "Files" or "User Files."

"User Files" are sometimes called by the name of the program they're used with. For example, a "Word File" is a file that's used with the "Word Program." Likewise, a "Graphics File" is one that's used with a graphics program like "Photo Shop."

Earlier you learned how to find a file using the "Find" window, and then you discovered how to read the path leading to that file. The path gave you a road map to the location of a file on your hard disk.

Files are put into a series of folders. This is how Windows organizes the disk drives on your computer. You should always try to develop your own "map" or "path" when you create files. That way you can avoid confusion when you need to find a specific file.

A. More options

Double click on the "My Computer" icon and then on your C: drive. Now you'll see a list of folders and files that are on that drive. Take a look at the window right below the title bar. You should see some words that present options for customizing this window.

First, maximize the C: drive window.

Next, click on "View." A list drops down with several options. Toward the middle of it you should see the following options.

• Large Icons

• Small Icons

• List

• Details

Note: In Windows XP, you may see additional options. For now ignore them.

One of these selections will have a black dot (a bullet) next to it. This indicates that you're currently using this option. When Windows is set up for the first time, the setting is "Large Icons." If this is what's been selected, try moving the pointer over the "Small Icons" option and left clicking once.

You should see the same files and folders in the window, but the icons (pictures) are much smaller, so more of them fit into the window.

"Small Icons" look just like "Large Icons" except that they're smaller. If you have a hard time seeing the icons in your window, use the "Large Icons" option.

Now click on "View" and select "List." At first glance, it looks a lot like the "Small Icons" option, but notice that the order of the folders and files is different. Instead of being arranged across the top, they're now arranged into columns.

Finally, click on "View" and select "Details" from the options. What you see may resemble the "List" option, but notice that other information is now displayed. There are new columns called "Size," "Type," and "Modified."

If you need to know how large a file is, or when you last worked on it, this is a great option.

If you are using Microsoft Windows 98 or Windows 2000, now would be a good time to double check some of your Windows settings to make sure that the windows on your computer look like the ones shown in this book.

1. Double click on the "My Computer" icon on your desktop.

2. In the window that opens click once on the word 'View'.

3. Move the pointer over the "Toolbars" option and a new set of options will appear.

4. There should be check marks next to the following options "Standard Buttons" "Address Bar" and "Text Labels". If there isn't a check mark next any of these options, move the cursor over the item and left click on it.

Exercise #13
Describe the following

Explain how windows organizes the stuff on your hard drive and other disks?

_____

_____

_____

B. Creating a folder

The first step in organizing your work is to create a folder. You can create as many folders as you wish.

For now, let's create a folder in your C: drive and give it your first name.

To create a folder on a disk you need to be looking at the disk itself. So double click on "My Computer" and then double click on the C: drive.

1. Put the pointer over the word "File" right under the title bar and left click once.

2. In the list that appears, put the pointer over the word "New." Hold it there for a second or two.

3. A new set of options will appear. At the top will be "Folder." Slide the pointer over the word folder and left click.

4. Notice that something called "New Folder" shows up in the window.

This is a great start! But we wanted to give the folder your first name, not the boring name of "New Folder."

Here's how to rename the folder.

1. Left click once on the new folder. It should become highlighted.

2. Put the pointer on top of the word "File" under the title bar of the window and left click once.

3. In the list that drops down select "Rename." When you do this the text portion of the "New Folder" will be highlighted and a box will be drawn around it.

4. To rename the folder just start typing in your first name. As you do, the name of the folder will change. If you make any mistakes just use the backspace key and correct them.

5. When you're done typing in your name, press the "Enter" key on your keyboard.

That's all there is to it. Double click on the folder with your name on it. When the new window opens, it should be empty. That's because you've just created this folder and you haven't yet put anything into it.

Now create another folder called "Letters." If you are unsure how to do this, follow the same steps listed above, except this time name the folder "Letters."

If you want to practice making folders, go ahead. Just create another folder in this window and call it "Practice." Then double click on the "Practice" folder and make as many folders in that folder as you wish.

When you're done practicing, just close all the windows and continue on.

C. Creating a file

You just made a folder. Now you're going to make a file.

64

In order to make a file you need to use a program. All sorts of programs can help you create files. Word processing programs create files for your letters, notes, and similar items. Games save files so that you can continue playing the game precisely where you left off.

Now you're going to create a simple file using a program that's included with Windows. It's called "Notepad," and all it does is save files containing material you've typed. It doesn't have any spell-checking abilities or formatting options. It's very basic.

But in Windows, the process of saving a file with "Notepad" is the same as the one used in an elaborate and expensive program. So why not learn the process with a simple program?

To run "Notepad" follow these directions:

1. Click on the "Start" button.

2. Put the pointer over the "Programs" option. In Windows XP put the pointer over the "All Programs" option.

3. When a list of options pops up, put the pointer over "Accessories."

4. When a new list of options pops up, move the pointer to "Notepad" and left click.

A new window called "Untitled – Notepad" will open. All this means is that you're working on the computer's equivalent of a blank sheet of paper. Start to type something in the window. If you don't know how to type, just press some keys and fill up a few lines in the window with some text.

Let's assume that you're working on a file represented by this typing. It's late at night, you're tired, and you want to go to bed. If you're lazy, you could just leave your computer on. But that would be very risky. If the power goes off in the middle of the night or if someone else decides to touch your keyboard, your work could be lost forever.

The best thing to do in this situation is to save your work onto your hard disk so that you can continue to work on it later. To save your work, simply move the pointer over the word "File" and left click once. A drop down list will appear. Put your pointer over the word "Save." Then left click once.

As soon as you do this, a special box called the "Save As" box will open up. You'll use this box just about every time you need to save a program. Take a look at the parts of this window. You should become very comfortable using it.

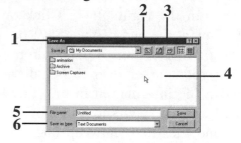

Save As Box

The main parts you should know are:

1. Save in: This is a window that shows where you're saving the file. Click on the down arrow at the end of this box. A drop down list of all the drives connected to your computer will appear.

2. Up One Level: If you double click on the wrong folder, you can click on this gadget to go back up one folder. You can do this several times, going up one folder at a time.

3. Create New Folder: If you forgot to make a folder for your letters, you could make it by clicking on this gadget.

4. File list box: This is a window showing the contents of the folder you're looking in.

5. File name: This is where you tell Windows what you want to call the new file.

6. Save as type: This is a small window that gives you options as to what type of file you are saving. For now it should read "Text."

Documents." If you want to see other options, click on the down arrow at the end of this box. Your options will change depending on what program you're using and the type of file you're working with. Make sure it's set back to "Text Documents" before you save.

Chances are that "Notepad" has already chosen a place to save your file. Before you save it, you should make sure you're putting it in the right place. Click on the down arrow at the end of the "Save In" line. Look at the list of things in the drop down box. Put your cursor over the C: drive and left click. The information in the "File List" box will change. You should recognize the folders and files that show up now. They're the same ones you'd see if you had double clicked on "My Computer" and then double clicked on the C: drive.

Remember a few steps back when you created a folder and gave it your first name? You should see this folder somewhere in the list. When you find it, double click on it. A new list of items will show up. Notice how the top information box has changed too. It now has your first name as the name of the folder. You should also see other folders. One should say "Letters." Double click on this folder. You're now in the letters folder, and you can verify this by looking at the name displayed in the "Save In" box.

Right now the file name is "Untitled." You need to change this. Put the pointer over "Untitled" and left click once. A blinking vertical cursor will appear in the box. This means the computer is waiting for you to enter a name. But first you need to erase the old name. Press and hold the right pointing arrow on your keyboard until the blinking cursor is at the end of the word "Untitled."

Then press and hold the backspace key on your keyboard until the name is erased. Type in the name you've chosen. For this example type in "First". Then press the "Enter" key on the keyboard or click on the "Save" button.

Either by pressing the "Enter" key on the keyboard or by clicking on the "Save" button, you've just saved your file to the hard disk. It happens very quickly. All you're likely to see is the window close and the "Notepad" window come back to the top.

There is one small change, though. Take a look at the title bar. You'll notice that it now contains the name you chose instead of "Untitled."

You should know a few other things about saving files. For instance, you can have only one file of a particular name in any one folder.

Windows automatically warns you if you're saving a file with the same name as another file. If you tell Windows it's okay to do so, Windows will erase (delete) the old file and put the new one in its place. Once the old file has been replaced, there's no going back to it. So when Windows asks you if you really want to do this, make sure you know what you're doing. If you carelessly click "Yes" or "OK" in response to this question, you may be getting rid of something you'll need later.

The best policy is to answer "No" to the question asking if you really want to replace the file with the same name. Then go back and choose a different name. In Windows 95, Windows 98 and Windows 2000 file names don't have to be short. You can name a letter you write to a friend, "Letter to John about golf."

Generally, keep file names as short as possible. That way, you'll be able to find them more easily later on. But don't take this advice to the extreme. File names like "A" or "jsid" quickly become meaningless. You can name your files anything you want.

If you were a salesperson and you wanted to keep track of letters you sent to clients with the name of John, what would you do if you had a number of Johns you wrote to? If you understand the problem created by this situation, chances are you can see why it's crucial also to understand the organization of the Windows file system.

One way to solve the problem I've described would be to create more folders inside the "Letters" folder. You could create one folder called "John Bebell" and another called "John Denyse." Now you could keep letters for each John in the folders labeled with their first and last names.

Let's now make sure that the file you saved really got saved. Close all the windows that are open, including the "Notepad." Can you remember where you saved the file? Many new users have problems with this. They can save files fine, but they can't find them. So they may think that the file was never saved. Actually, it's just lost among the thousands of other files and folders on your hard disk.

Can you think of a way to find your file?

If you forgot where you put the file, why not try the "Find" window located under the "Start" button? All you have to do is remember what you called it—or at least a part of its name—and then click the "Find Now" button.

Or you could double click on "My Computer," then double click again on the C: drive and poke around to see if you can find it that way.

If you can't remember where your file is, this is how to get to where it was saved.

1. Double click on "My Computer."

2. Double click on the C: drive.

3. Double click on the folder with your name.

4. Double click on the "Letters" folder.

5. Now you should see a file called "First."

Note: Even though the name of the "First" file is just that, you may see something like "First.txt" in the window. That's okay. Windows will sometimes put a dot and a three-letter description of the file after it. This is for Windows' own information, so don't change it.

The ".txt" part of the name tells Windows that the file is a text file and can be used with "Notepad." If you remove this part of the name, Windows will no longer know what program this file goes with.

But you can completely ignore the ".txt" part of the file name. As far as you're concerned, the file name is simply "First."

If for some reason you don't see the file, go to the "Find" window and do a search on your hard disk for the file. If you get several results, try to narrow the search by looking only for the files that start with "first." You can do this by typing "first*" in the search box.

If you're still unable to find the file, start "Notepad" again, make a new file and save it. Pay close attention to the "Save" dialog box and to where you're saving the file. You'll have to change the folders from the ones that "Notepad" starts out with.

Assuming you found the file, take a look at it in the window. You'll notice that the icon for this file looks like a sheet of paper with some writing on it. Every type of file has its own special icon. As you use Windows more and more, you'll be able to identify quickly what's in a file just by looking at its icon.

Exercise #14
Name the parts

1. _____

2. _____

3. _____

4. _____

5. _____

6. _____

D. Loading a file

Close that window and run "Notepad" again. As usual, it'll start out with a blank sheet of paper. At this time you'd like to continue working on the letter you started earlier. How can you do this?

Whenever you want to continue where you left off, you need to load a file, also referred to as opening a file. When you do this, the program loads the file you saved into the computer and shows it to you. You can either start typing where you left off, or you can revise the letter.

Loading a file in "Notepad" is very similar to loading a file in any other program. The option to load or open a file is almost always under the "File" part of the menu, which is located just under the windows title bar.

Put the pointer on top of the word "File" and left click on it. In the list that pops up, find the option labeled "Open" and left click on it. In some programs the option will be called "Load."

When you click on the "Open" option, a new window opens up. It's the "Open" window box, and it's exactly like the "Save" window box. All the parts work just like they do in the "Save" window box, except now the "Save" button is labeled "Open" and at the top the input box is labeled "Look in:."

To find and load your file, you'll have to use the "Open" window to display the folder containing the file you want to load. Left click once on that file. Finally, click on the "Open" button.

Here's the step-by-step way to find and load your file.

1. Left click once on the down arrow at the end of the "Look in:" box.

2. Find the C: drive in the list that pops up and left click once on it.

3. In the window below the "Look in:" box, find the folder with your name and double click on it.

4. Double click on the "Letters" folder.

5. Click on the file "First" so that it's highlighted.

6. Click on the "Open" button.

Note: If you wish, you can change step 5 into a double click on the file "First." This would load the program. It's just another variation.

After you click the "Open" button, the window will disappear and the "Notepad" window will be on top again. The title bar of the program will have the name 'First' in it. Below that, in the typing window, you'll see the work you did earlier.

E. Making changes

You've loaded in a file and can now change or add to it. Click somewhere on the text so that you have the blinking vertical bar, called a cursor. Using the up, down, left, or right pointing arrows on the keyboard, move the cursor around until you get to the end of the typed material.

Press return a few times to add some blank lines to the bottom of the old stuff you typed. Now type in some new text. When you're done you'll want to save your changes.

F. Saving your file again

To save the file you've changed, just click once on the "File" option and then once on the "Save" option. This time you'll notice that the program didn't bring up a "Save" window box. In fact, you may have gotten the impression that nothing at all happened.

Since you loaded the file in, Windows remembered where you loaded it in from as well as the file name. When you clicked on "Save" Windows just did all the work for you.

If for some reason you wanted to save the file under a different name while leaving the first file alone, you could do that by choosing the "Save as" option listed just under the "Save" option. Go ahead and try this out. Make some more changes to the text in your window and then save the file again using the "Save as" option. When you do the "Save" window box will open.

Make sure you change to the folder with your name and then to the letters folder. Then change the name of the file in the name input box and click on the "Save" button.

You now have two files. One is the original "First" file, and the other is your second file with the changes you made. You should also notice that the name in the title bar has now changed to the new name you typed in. Windows now thinks this is the file you'll be working with and will automatically remember the name and the folder to save it in until you change it again.

If you want to load in the older version of your file, just click on "File" and then on "Open" to open the file.

Let's try one more experiment. Start typing something in the window. When you're done, try closing the program by clicking on the close gadget. What happens?

Windows has warned you that the text in the file has been changed, and it's asking you if you want to save those changes before you quit the program. Windows is giving you a last chance to keep your work before you quit the program. Consider it a little safety net.

If you don't save the changes, anything you did to the file since the last time you changed it will be lost when you close the file.

If the window asking you if you want to save the changes is still on your computer, click "No." The "Notepad" program will close. Close all other windows or programs that are open so you can see the desktop.

G. Renaming a file

What happens if you save a file and later want to rename it something else? Windows has two quick and easy ways to let you do this. We've already gone over one way earlier when you were creating new folders. Don't worry if you can't remember. You'll get a brief refresher in this section, and you'll also learn a new way to rename files.

Open up the window of the folder with your name on it. If you don't know how, here are the steps.

1. Double click on "My Computer."

2. Double click on the C: drive.

3. Double click on the folder with your name on it.

You should see a folder called "Letters" and, if you did the practice section on creating folders, you should also have a "Practice" folder. Double click on the "Letters" folder, and then left click on one of the files you see in the window. Now click on the word "File" at the top of the window and select "Rename" from the list.

As you can see, you rename files in exactly the same way that you rename folders. But there's one thing you have to keep in mind.

You may recall that on some computers, file names in a window may have what are called file name extensions. Thus, a text file may look like "filename.txt." The extension tells Windows how to use that file.

If your computer is showing you extensions on the end of the file name, you must keep them in the name when you rename the file. That's all you ever have to know about extensions. Just leave them alone.

So in the example above, if you were renaming a file that was showing up on your computer as "First.txt," you'd do the following:

1. Click once on the file to select it.

2. Click the word "File" near the top of the window.

3. Type a new name for the file, making sure you also put the ".txt" extension at the end. For example: "new name.txt" or "new.txt."

4. Press the "Enter" key on the keyboard.

If you forget to add the extension or if you mistype it, you'll get a warning box from Windows. Just click "No" to the question "Are you sure you want to make these changes?" Then start over.

If you've started to type the name and have forgotten to take note of the extension, you can hit the "Esc" key (Escape) on your keyboard. This puts the file name back to the way it was and you can start over.

H. Moving files from place to place

Sometimes you might accidentally put a file in the wrong place. Or sometimes you might just want to move a file to another place. If for any reason you want to move files or folders around, Windows makes it easy.

In order to make sure you get the same results on your computer as I have in the examples in this section, you'll have to check out a few settings in your windows. If you want, you can always change the settings back after this section. Just write down your settings on a sheet of paper, and when you're finished with this section go back and change them.

Windows 95 only:

To determine whether you need to make these changes, perform the following test.

1. Double click on "My Computer" and a window should open.

2. Now double click on the C: drive.

When you double clicked on the C: drive, did a new window open up giving you two open windows?

If your computer just replaced the contents of the "My Computer"' window with the contents of the C: drive, leaving only one window in the task bar, you don't have to make any changes.

If you got two windows, make the following changes.

Windows 95 only

1. Close all programs and windows so that you see only the desktop.

2. Double click on "My Computer."

3. Towards the top of the window under the title bar, find the word "View" and click once on it.

---

4. Now click on the bottom option, which is called "Options."

5. In the window that opens, make sure the bottom option, "Browse folders by using a single window that changes as you open each folder," is selected by clicking on the button to the left of it.

6. Click on "OK."

Now just check one more setting. Click on the "View" option again and make sure there's a check mark next to the "Toolbar" option. If there isn't, click on the "Toolbar" option. This will make some icons appear below the title bar.

In Windows 98, Windows Me, Windows 2000 and Windows XP you have to make sure of just a few settings.

1. Click on the "View" option.

2. Put the pointer over the "Toolbars" option.

3. Make sure there's a check mark next to Standard Buttons." If there isn't click on it. When you do this the options list will close. Go back and click on "View," and then put the pointer over the "Toolbars" option.

4. Make sure there's a check mark next to "Address Bar." If there isn't, click on it. When you do this the options list will close. Go back and click on "View" and then put the pointer over the "Toolbars" option.

Skip this 5 if you are using Windows XP

5. Make sure there's a check mark next to "Text Labels." If there isn't, click on it.

This will make some icons appear under the title bar.

Make sure that all windows are closed and no programs are running. Then open the window showing the contents of the "Letters" folder.

If you're not sure, here's how to do it:

1. Double click on "My Computer."

2. Double click on the C: drive.

3. Double click on the folder with your name.

4. Double click on the "Letter" folder

Did you notice that this time when you opened the windows they all opened in the same window? Sometimes when you're looking for a file you can have many windows open, cluttering your desktop and your task bar. This option helps to eliminate the clutter.

At this time you should see two files, "First" and "Second," the two you made in the last section with "Notepad." If you don't see them or if one is missing, go back to that section and follow the directions to make them.

Let's say you want to move the "Second" file out of the "Letters" folder and into the folder with your name. The simplest way to do this is to just drag and drop the file into the folder you want to put it in. But you can't see the folder with your name because you're within a folder inside of that folder.

Look at your desktop. If you can't see the "My Computer" icon, grab the window you have open and move it to another corner of the screen so that you can see the "My Computer" icon.

Then do the following:

1. Double click on the "My Computer" icon.

2. Double click on the C: drive.

3. Double click on the folder with your name.

You should see two windows now. One window is the "Letters" folder and the other window is the folder with your name. You can tell what folder you are looking at by the name in the title bar.

If you don't see two windows, they're probably right on top of each other. Just grab one of the windows and move it out of the way. The one below will become visible.

If both windows don't fit on the screen, resize them so that you can see both of them at the same time.

Now put the pointer over the "Second" file and click on it once to highlight it. Click again on the file, but this time hold the button. (Don't click too soon after the first click you used to highlight the file. If you do, the computer may think you wanted to double click.)

If for some reason you accidentally double clicked on the file and "Notepad" opened up, just close "Notepad" and try again.

Now, while you're holding the button down, drag the file out of the "Letters" folder and into the folder with your name. Then release the button.

You've now moved the file out of one folder and into another. Notice how it's no longer in the "Letters" folder.

I. Making a copy

There's another trick you can do easily. If you want to make a copy of the "First" file in another directory, that's as easy to do as moving a file was.

Click once on the "First" file to select it. Now click and hold the left mouse button down and drag this file out into the folder with your name on it.

Before you let go of the mouse, press down and hold the "Control" key on your keyboard. Sometimes this key is labeled "Ctrl," and it's usually in the lower left corner of the keyboard.

When you hold the "Control" key down a little plus (+) symbol will appear next to the file you're dragging. If you don't see it, release the "Control" key and press it a few times so you can see the plus symbol flash.

With the "Control" key still pressed down, release the left mouse button. This will copy the file into the folder with your name on it. You should see the "First" file in both of the windows.

If you accidentally moved the "First" file into the folder with your name on it, just try copying it into the "Letters" folder by using the above technique.

You can move and copy folders this way too. If you move a folder, everything in that folder will move or be copied with it.

J. Copying files to a floppy disk

Copying files from your computer to a floppy disk is as easy as moving files from one folder to another. Here's the basic process:

First, find the file you want to copy to the floppy disk. Click your mouse pointer on the file and drag it to the floppy disk. It's that easy. Let's try.

Now, you'll need a floppy disk that is formatted and ready to use. If the disk doesn't work with this example, you can try another disk or refer to the section on floppy disks to make sure the disk is formatted.

Put the floppy disk into the disk drive. Then double click on the "My Computer" icon on your desktop and then double click on the "A:" drive. This will open a window on your computer that shows you what is on your floppy disk. If you have files on that floppy disk, they will be displayed in this window. If the disk is blank, you will not see anything in this window.

Now you need to find a file to copy. If you need to, you can first move the floppy drive window, but don't close it. Then, double click on the "My Computer" icon on your desktop again. Now double click on your "C:" drive and then double click on the folder with your name on it. Double click on the letters folder and find one of the sample files we created earlier in this book.

Make sure that you can see on your desktop both the floppy drive ("A:") window and the window with the file you that want to copy. Move those windows around or resize them if you want.

Now, click and then drag the icon of the sample file into the floppy window.

If you did this correctly, you should see an icon appear in the floppy drive window in a few seconds.

There is another way to copy files or folders to a floppy disk. Find another sample letter in your letters folder. If you need to, you can make a sample letter with Notepad and save it. When you find the file you want to copy, RIGHT click one time on its icon. A short list will pop up. Put the mouse pointer over the "Send To" option. Another list will appear and one of the choices will be "3 _ Floppy (A:)". Put the mouse pointer over this option and left click on it. The file will be automatically copied to the floppy drive and the disk in that drive.

These are simply two different ways to do the same task.

Keep in mind that floppy disks have a small amount of space and can't hold a lot of files, or very large files. If you get an error message stating the disk is out of space or that it is full, you can try to delete any unneeded files off the floppy disk. If this doesn't help, the file or files are probably too large to fit on a floppy.

If you have a Zip disk drive on your computer, you can save many more files, and larger files, than you can on a floppy. The drive letter for a Zip drive will not be "A:" It will likely be something like "S:" or some other letter.

You would copy files to a Zip disk in your Zip drive the very same way as I showed you above. The one exception is that you might not be able to use the right click and "send to option" to copy files onto a Zip disk.

You can manage your files and folders contained on a floppy disk just like you do on your internal hard disk. If you want to delete something, simply drag it to the "Recycle Bin" or click on it once and press the delete key.

One word of caution: Unlike your internal hard disk, when you delete something from a floppy disk or Zip disk, you cannot retrieve it from the "Recycle Bin". Once you delete off a floppy disk or Zip disk, the file or folder is gone forever. Be careful.

K. Shortcuts

Now close all windows and programs except the window with the "First" file in it. If you don't have any windows open, open the "Letter" folder.

Sometimes you'll be working with a particular folder, file or program a lot. It's annoying to have to go looking through Windows each time, looking for the file, folder or program you want to work with.

It would be much handier if you could just have the file, folder or program on your desktop so you could double click on it quickly. You might be in the habit of keeping certain files out of the filing cabinet and on your desk while you're working on them.

But if you simply copied the files, folders or programs to your desktop, you'd be undermining the file organization on your hard disk. So what can you do?

In Windows you can create a shortcut, which is like a pointer. You can make a shortcut for any file, folder or program on your computer. When you do this, the file, folder or program stays exactly where it was. You're not copying or moving it.

A new icon will appear on your desktop. When you double click on it, your computer will go to the folder where the file, folder or program is located and open a window for it.

You should have on your screen the window with the "First" file in it. You should also be able to see some of the desktop around the window. If you can't, then resize the window so that you can.

To create a shortcut to the "First" file on your desktop, follow these steps:

1. Left click once on the "First" file to select it.

2. Now RIGHT click on the file and hold the right mouse button down.

3. Drag the file out onto an empty area of the desktop and release the right mouse button.

4. Left click on the "Create Shortcut(s) Here" option that pops up.

A new shortcut will be put on your desktop. Now close all the windows and programs you may have open.

The new icon on your desktop should be called "Shortcut to First," and it'll be placed in the spot where you released the right mouse button. If you want to move it, just left click, drag it to a new spot, and release the button.

Now double click on the shortcut, and "Notepad" opens the file for you. This is quite handy if you're working a lot on one file.

Since you seem to be going to the folder with your name on it, why don't you create a shortcut to it? That way you won't have to double click on "My Computer" and then double click on the C: drive and so on.

Here's how to do it.

To make a shortcut to the folder with your name on it do the following:

1. Double click on "My Computer."

2. Double click on the C: drive.

3. Find the folder with your name on it.

Left click just once to select it. Remember, clicking twice will open it. You just want to highlight it by clicking once.

4. Now, right click, hold the button down, and drag the folder to an empty area of the desktop.

5. Release the mouse button and choose "Create Shortcut Here" from the options.

Did you notice that two other options popped up when you released the right mouse button?

• Move Here

• Copy Here

These options will also let you move and copy files, folders and programs — more examples of how you can do things several different ways in Windows.

If you had right clicked and dragged a file by accident, you could have chosen the "Cancel" option to keep anything from happening that you didn't want to happen.

In Windows, if you're ever uncertain, or if you get to a place where you don't know what you're doing, just hit "Cancel" and nothing will happen, no changes will be made.

L. Deleting a file

What do you do when you're done with a file forever and you want to get rid of it? You have to delete it.

Deleting files is easy in Windows. Sometimes too easy. If you want to delete a file just click on it and drag it onto the "Recycle Bin" (the trash can on your desktop). When you hold the file over the trash can icon, the trash can becomes highlighted. And when you release the mouse button, Windows will ask, "Are you sure you want to send "File name" to the "Recycle Bin?" If you click on "Yes," the file will disappear into the "Recycle Bin."

Try this with the shortcut you just created. Grab the "Shortcut to First" and drag it on top of the trash can on your desktop. Then release the button and answer "Yes" when you're asked if you want to send the file to the Recycle Bin. If you did this correctly, the shortcut will no longer be visible on the desktop.

If the "Recycle Bin" was empty, did you notice that the icon of the trash can seemed to fill up when you put the shortcut in? This is a visual indicator that there are things inside the "Recycle Bin."

Later you'll learn more about the "Recycle Bin."

There's another way to delete a file. This method is good when you have a large window open and you can't see the "Recycle Bin." Simply left click once on the file, folder or program to highlight what you want to delete. Then press the "Delete" key on your keyboard. Windows will ask "Are you sure you want to send "First" (or whatever the name of your file is) to the Recycle Bin?" Click "Yes." Poof. The file's gone. You deleted it without having to drag it to the 'Recycle Bin'.

Now, delete the "Practice" folder if you created it. Otherwise, create a practice folder and then try deleting it.

M. Using the trash can

Recycle Bin

In the previous section you dragged some files and folders into the "Recycle Bin" and they disappeared from view. If the "Recycle Bin" was empty, the icon of the trash can appeared to fill up when you put the first file in.

The "Recycle Bin" is a special part of Windows. It's very much like a real trash can,

a place where you put everything you want to get rid of. And, like a real trash can, it'll fill up. If you ever throw something out and want to get it back, you simply reach into the trash can and pull it out, right? The same holds true with the "Recycle Bin."

To see how this works, let's delete another file, one that we'll want back. Open the window for the folder with your name. You should see the "Second" file and the "Letters" folder. Inside the "Letters" folder is the "First" file.

What would happen if you highlighted the "Letters" folder and pressed the "Delete" key on your keyboard?

Try it. Then answer "Yes" to the question Windows asks you. The folder goes away, and with it goes the "First" file too. Remember that when you move, copy, or delete a folder, everything inside that folder will be moved, copied or deleted as well.

But now you need to get the folder back. Close all windows. Put your pointer over the "Recycle Bin" and double click on it.

A new window will open and you'll see the contents of the "Recycle Bin." If you look through the list, sure enough, you'll find the "Letters" folder. In the next column titled "Original Location," you can see the path that the folder was in. You can also see the date you deleted the file in the next column, "Date Deleted." All the other familiar information is there, like "Type" and "Size."

Left click once to highlight the "Letters" folder, and then right click on it. Some options pop up in a box. The top one is called "Restore." When you put the pointer over this option and left click, the folder will disappear from the "Recycle Bin."

Close all windows and then double click on the shortcut you created to the folder with your name. You'll now see the "Letters" folder safely back where it was before you deleted it.

Actually, then, when you move something to the "Recycle Bin," you aren't quite deleting it yet. The "Recycle Bin" is an intermediate step in the deletion process. It gives you one last chance to get the file back.

N. Emptying the trash can

Close all windows. It's time to get rid of those files in the "Recycle Bin" for good, for real.

Right click on the "Recycle Bin" and an option list will pop up. Left click on the one called "Empty Recycle Bin."

This time Windows asks "Are you sure you want to delete these items?" You're quite close to the point of no return. When you answer "Yes" to this question, all the items in the "Recycle Bin" will be deleted. Permanently. You won't ever be able to get them back.

When you remove old unneeded files, you free up space on your hard disk — or on any other disk the file was on. This is important to keep in mind. You can fill up your computer with junk files and programs quickly if you aren't careful. Try not to keep extra copies of files around. When you do finish with something that you won't be using again, get it off your hard disk.

If it's something too important to get rid of forever, you can back it up (make a copy of it) onto a floppy disk. There are also other ways to backup or keep archival copies of files so they won't take up space on your hard disk.

But you don't want to go to the opposite extreme either. In a later section you'll learn how to tell how much space is left on your hard disk and how to remove programs from your computer safely.

One last tip about using the "Recycle Bin." If you can, when you put files there, you should leave them there for a day or so. That way, if you throw away something that affects how your computer works, you can get it back.

For example, let's say that you decide you no longer need a folder containing some files or even some programs. You'd put the folder and its contents into the "Recycle Bin" and leave them there for a day or so. This will give you a chance to see how your computer shuts down and starts up. You also will have had a chance to run other programs and to see whether anything on your computer has been affected.

If you notice that some of the computer's functions aren't working quite the same as they were, you can go into the "Recycle Bin" and restore all the files you deleted. That should bring your computer back to the way it was.

If you don't notice anything different about your computer and all your programs work fine, you can probably empty the "Recycle Bin" and delete the files for good.

This policy isn't foolproof. The best and safest policy is, if you don't know what something is, leave it alone. There are some folders and files you should never mess with. They are:

- Program Files
- Windows
- Autoexec or Autoexec.bat
- Config or Config.sys or Config.dos
- Command or Command.com

These folders and files contain vital information your computer needs in order to run. If you get rid of them or move them around, your computer may not work and may need to have some work performed on it.

O. Floppy disks

Finally, you should know something about floppy disks. In may ways they're very much like hard disks. The major difference is that sometimes you may have to format them. It's possible to put a new floppy disk into your computer, double click on the A: drive in "My Computer," and have the computer give you an error message. Most likely, the disk isn't formatted.

To format a disk, follow these steps:

1. Insert the floppy disk into the drive.

2. Double click on "My computer."

3. Right click on the A: drive.

4. Choose the "Format" option from the list that pops up.

In the format window that opens, you can choose the size. You should usually leave this option alone.

Next is the type of format. Choose "Quick" if you just want to erase the disk. If you can't read the disk, you should do a "Full" format.

Then just click the "Start" button and wait while the disk is being formatted.

There's one part of a floppy disk you should know about. If you flip the disk over and look in the upper left corner you'll see a little black plastic piece that can slide up and down. If you slide the plastic piece up you'll make a hole in the disk that you can see through. If you slide the piece down it will cover up the hole in the disk.

This is called the "write protect" tab. By sliding this tab up or down you can protect a disk from being accidentally erased or having an important file deleted from it.

If you slide the tab down so that you cannot see through it, you can then save and delete files to and from the disk. You can also format the disk.

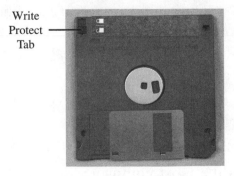

Write Protect Tab

Floppy Disk

If you slide the tab up so that there's a hole in it, you won't be able to save or delete files. And you won't be able to format the disk either. The disk is protected and all you can do is look at the material on it.

VII.
Printers

A printer is a machine that attaches to your computer and puts the words and images on your screen onto paper.

Printers come in many different flavors. Some print in color, while others are strictly black and white. Some are like copy machines and use lasers and toner to draw the images on the paper. Others use ink cartridges and spray the ink onto the page. Older printers used ribbons much as typewriters did.

Since I can't possibly cover dozens of printers in the hope of talking about the one you may own, I'll stick to basic concepts that should apply to all printers. Always refer to the specific instructions that came with your system and/or printer.

To set up a printer for Windows to use, you need to get into the printer window. To do so, follow these steps:

In Windows XP:

1. Click on the "Start" button.

2. Click on "Printers and Faxes"

In all other versions of Windows:

1. Double click on "My Computer"

2. Double click on "Printers"

You'll see a list of the printers that have been set up on your computer. If you have fax software installed with your modem, you'll also see the fax machine here too. Windows treats a fax machine just like a printer.

If you don't see your printer listed here, click on "Add Printer" to start the setup of your printer. From here on, the process will for the most part be automatic. You should have handy the disks or CDs that came with your printer. They have the information you'll need to complete the setup of the printer.

Once the printer is set up properly, you'll see it in the list of printers on your computer. Double click on the icon of your printer.

You'll see the printer window. It displays a list of any documents that you may be sending to the printer as well as the task the printer is currently working on. You can also locate a print job that you sent to your printer and stop it or cancel it if you want.

Click on the word "Printer" at the top of the window just below the title bar. If this is your only printer, there should be a check mark next to "Set as Default Printer." If your printer is currently printing something, you can select "Pause Printing" in order to stop printing.

If you want, you can "Purge Print Documents." This deletes all the current documents the printer is printing.

If the printer is currently working on several documents, they'll be listed in the bottom half of this window. You can click once on a print job that's listed to select it. Then you can click on the word "Document" at the top of the window under the title bar to pause or cancel this particular print job.

When you're done with this window close it.

VIII.
Scanners

Scanners are handy devices that attach to your computer. You can use the scanner to "take a picture" of photographs, drawings, and similar documents. Then you can load these into your computer.

All the scanner does is make a graphic picture for your computer of any object you place into it. You can place anything into your scanner that you could place into a copy machine. Most all scanners are color, so unlike a copy machine you can get a full color picture of things on your computer.

Some scanners will also let you scan transparencies, negatives and slides. You should check your scanner's instructions to find out just what it can do.

As is true with printers, all scanners are different and hundreds of different makes and models are sold. Refer to your scanner's instructions for setup and operation. This text will describe basic concepts that should be applicable for most scanners. Your own software and screens may be different from those described in this text.

To scan something you'll need a graphics program. One should have been included with your scanner. Although many differences exist between the many available graphics programs, they all operate in similar fashion. Every time you scan something you'll go through these steps on your computer.

1. Put the object you want to scan into the scanner and close the lid.

2. Start your graphics program and find the scan option.

3. Scan the object using the scanner's software.

4. Edit the graphic (the scan) with the graphics program.

5. Save the graphic to your hard disk.

Perhaps the most confusing steps listed above are numbers two and five.

In step two you'll have to play around with the graphics software that came with your scanner. Most graphics programs have an option under "File" called "import" or "acquire" or perhaps "twain" or even "scan."

If you see "twain source" or "twain 32," these may be your scanner. Many graphics programs use the word "twain" or "twain 32" to mean scanner. It sounds stupid, and it's a bit misleading, but that's the way it is. It's one of those things that should be changed but hasn't been.

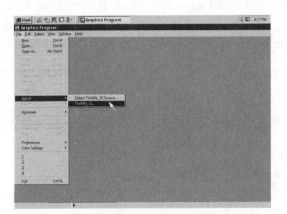

Twain 32 Option

When you find the scan option in your graphics program, it'll most likely give control of your scanner to another program that came with the scanner. This special scanner program lets you preview what you put on the scanner before you really scan it.

A preview is a quick look at what's in the scanner. What you see won't be of very high quality. You're only looking to make sure that the object you put in the scanner is straight and that it all fits on the scanner.

You can draw a rectangle around the area of the preview you want to scan. That area can be a part of the object or the whole object. When you draw the rectangle the edges will look like a moving dotted line. This line is sometimes called marching ants because it looks like little ants are marching around the object you select.

Once you get the preview to look the way you want it to, hit the "Scan" button to start scanning the object you've put in it. Once it's done scanning, the special scanning software should exit. If it doesn't, click on close or exit, to get back to the graphics program. You should now be placed back into your graphics program so that you can edit and save the scan.

There are lots of ways you can edit your scan with a graphics program. You can take out smudges and touch up things. You can also adjust the color and contrast of the image so that it looks better. Then you can save the image in step five.

This can be confusing because if you don't save the image correctly, you may not be able to use it with other programs. As a general rule, you'll use only two types of graphics formats.

GIF, sometimes called CompuServe GIF, is a good graphics format that can be used with just about any program in the world.

JPG or JPEG is another graphics format that gives very good results and can be used with just about any program worldwide.

You'll have to tell your computer that you want to save the scan as one of these types. Many times you'll do this by selecting the file type at the bottom of the save box under the input box called "Save as:."

After you save the scan, you can quit your graphics program.

Scanners have a resolution that you can set just like you can set the resolution of Windows. Scanners express their resolution in dots per inch (dpi). Just like screen resolution, the higher the number the better the scan will look and print.

Scans can take up much space on your hard disk because they easily become very large. You should always scan at the lowest resolution you need. Play with different scanning resolutions to find what works best for your system. If you're going to send a picture (scan) to a friend on the Internet, you should scan it at 72 or 100 dots per inch (dpi). Yes, that sounds like a low resolution, but it could take you hours to send a bigger file. Keep it small when sending pictures over the Internet.

IX.
The Keyboard

In addition to the mouse, you can use the computer keyboard for all sorts of tasks, from typing letters to playing games.

Computer keyboards vary greatly, so I'll just go over the basics. Keep in mind that your personal keyboard may not have some of the keys described. You may even have other 'special' keys that aren't discussed here.

For the most part your computer keyboard is very much like an old typewriter keyboard. The letter, number, space, shift and caps lock keys all work the way you'd expect.

Take a closer look and you'll notice some special keys you may not recognize. Escape (Esc), Print Screen (Prt SC), Num Lock, and the F keys across the top of the keyboard, usually labeled F1 through F12, are all special keys used to give commands to the computer. These keys can act in many different ways, depending on the program that's running on the computer when you press them.

The escape key (Esc) is mainly used as a way of escaping from a program. For example, sometimes you may get into a place in a program that you don't want to be in. Or maybe you've selected an option you don't want. You can try pressing the Escape key to see if that will back you out or cancel the option. Keep in mind that this key doesn't always work. It depends on the program that you're running at the time.

The print screen key is the most puzzling for most people. Programs almost never support it, and when you press it nothing seems to happen. A long time ago when you wanted to print something on your printer, some programs would ask you to press Shift-Print Screen. Today no one seems to use the key. But it does do something.

Even though nothing seems to happen when you press the print screen key Windows takes a "snap shot" (picture) of the screen and every thing on it that you see. If you want to see this "snap shot" you'll need to use a program that lets you view graphics, like the paint program that comes with windows.

To see the Print Screen key in action try this exercise:

1. Close all programs and windows, and then press the Print Screen key.

2. Run the paint program.

   • Click on start

   • Put the pointer over "Programs" or "All Programs" if you're using Window XP

   • Put the pointer over accessories

   • Click on Paint

3. Click on the word 'Edit' at the top of the paint window.

4. Click on the word 'Paste' in the drop down list.

If a window pops up with the message "The image in the clipboard is larger than the bitmap. Would you like the bitmap enlarged?" Click 'Yes'.

You should see a picture of your screen in the paint program. This may not be something you use very often if at all. However, you're now one of the few people who actually know what the print screen key does.

The Num Lock key

On most computer keyboards there's a group of keys on the right that are separate from the rest of the keyboard. They are commonly used for entering numbers. People who are used to using business machines, calculators or cash registers are familiar with this key arrangement.

With practice you'll find that this numeric keypad is much quicker for typing numbers than the standard numbers across the top of the keyboard. It's particularly handy when you're using the calculator.

Look at the keys on the numeric keypad and you'll notice that some of them have words like home, end, and delete on them as well as numbers. This means that the keypad can function as either a numeric keypad (for typing numbers) or as a function keypad for use in other programs. The Num Lock key switches between these two modes. If you press the "5" key on the numeric keypad and nothing happens try pressing the Num Lock key and pressing "5" again.

As you press the Num Lock key you'll also notice a light goes on and off. This is similar to the Caps Lock light and helps you determine whether the Num Lock key has been pressed or not.

The function keys

Across the top of many keyboards is a row of keys labeled F1, F2, F3...F12. These are called Function keys, and for the most part they don't do anything. But if a programis designed to use them, they can be used to perform functions such as saving files, deleting characters, spell checking and other operations. Your best bet is to check with the instructions that came with the program you're using to see if it supports these keys.

One function key that's almost universally accepted is the F1 key. In most programs and in Windows this is the "help" function. If you press F1 in Windows, the "Windows Help" window will appear on your screen. There you can type in words and get general help about windows. The F1 help option also works in many other programs. If you ever get stuck, give it a try.

X.
Word Processing & Desktop Publishing

It wasn't long ago that you'd have to go to a professional to have a flyer laid out and printed. Thanks to the power of today's computers, you can do this from your home. To do the job properly, though, you'll need some tools such as the following:

- Software that does layout — like Microsoft Word or Publisher.

- Color printer with a good quality printout

- Scanner.

- Clipart.

You've already learned about the scanner and the printer, but what about the software? There are many good programs that make creating a flyer simple and easy. Because you could have any number of them, the techniques used in this section will be generic. Still, you should be able to form a mental image of the steps you need to follow in order to create a good flyer.

The first step is to have an idea of what you want to make. Let's say you're making a flyer to help sell your car.

Take a scan of a good photo of your car and save it as a JPEG or JPG file. Then open up your publishing software.

At the top in large type put "Car for $ale." And below that put the picture of your car.

Look at your program and find an option that will let you insert a graphic file. It's usually found under one of the options just beneath the title bar. Make sure to remember where you saved the file. Otherwise you may have to use the "Find" program under the "Start" button.

If your program will let you, try playing with different sizes of your picture and/or borders. Below that, in smaller type, put a description of you car.

Finally, in larger type, put in the price. Now save your work on your hard drive. It'll be there in case you want to make any changes in it at a later time.

Now print the flyer. If you click on the word "File," you'll see a list of options. In the lower part of the list, you'll see a print option. Click on it and your flyer should start to print out.

Cut and Paste

Say you're writing a letter on your computer and after several paragraphs you notice that some of your ideas are out of order. You decide you want to change the order of a few of the paragraphs.

You could type the whole letter again. But that would be a waste of time. Instead I suggest you use a very easy technique called: Cut and Paste.

Think of cutting as actually taking a pair of scissors and cutting the text out of the letter, if you had a printed letter in front of you. You do the same with the "Cut" command on your computer. (You actually electronically "Cut" the section away and store it temporarily in your computer!)

The second part of the command is "Paste." It is just as it sounds — you paste the cut material in the new spot you want it. It's the same as using your scissors and a jar of paste, except the computer does all the work.

It takes four steps to Cut and Paste:

1. First, you highlight (select) the text that you want to cut.

2. Second, you "Cut" the text out of your document.

3. Third, use either the mouse or your keyboard arrows to move your cursor to the point in your document where you want to put the text you just cut.

4. Fourth and last, you "Paste" (or put back) the text you cut into the new place you have chosen.

Let's try a quick experiment with a simple word processing program, called "Notepad," in your computer. If you don't remember how to open Notepad, here's what to do:

1. Click on the "Start" button.

2. Click on "Programs."

3. Click on "Accessories."

4. Click on "Notepad."

Start typing some text when the Notepad program window opens on your computer. Type at least five or six paragraphs so you have something to experiment with.

The first thing you want to do is highlight the text that you want to move. For this example, we want to take the last paragraph of your sample letter and move it to the beginning of the letter.

Move your mouse pointer to the beginning of the last paragraph, left click and, while holding onto that click, drag the mouse over the paragraph. You will want to drag both down and to the right to get the whole paragraph. As you do this, the text will become highlighted and look different from the rest of the text of the letter. When the entire paragraph is highlighted, let go of the mouse button.

If at first you miss some of the paragraph, don't worry. Just start over. Do this by clicking once on an area of your letter that is not highlighted. This will un-highlight the text, and then you can try again to highlight the last paragraph. (Simply repeat the steps above — after you try it a few times, you'll get the "feel" of highlighting text.)

Now, once you have the paragraph highlighted that you want to move, it is time to cut it out of your letter. There are two ways to do this. I'll show you both and you can decide which one you want to use.

The first way to cut text is to use the mouse. Move the pointer over the word "Edit" at the top of the "Notepad" window, and left click on "Edit." A short list will drop down. In that list you will see an option called "Cut." Click on that option. You'll notice your highlighted text will disappear. Don't worry. It is inside your computer on a place called the "Clipboard," waiting for you to paste it wherever you want.

Here is the second way to "Cut" your highlighted copy. You use your keyboard to do this. Once you've highlighted the text, press and hold the "Ctrl" key down and then press the "X" key on the keyboard. This key combination is called "Control-X". The control key is a special key that tells the computer you are giving it a command.

Again, you will see your highlighted text disappear and go to the "Clipboard."

Now, after you have cut your text, you are now ready to choose the spot to paste this text.

You need to move your cursor to the point in your letter where you want to put that cut text. Again, you can do this two ways. You can use the keyboard arrow keys to move your cursor to the point in the letter where you want to paste that text. Or use your mouse pointer to move to that point, and then left click once; this will move your cursor to that point.

Once you've chosen where you want to paste the text, you are now ready to actually paste it. As with cutting text out, you can do this two ways. I'll go over both methods and you can choose the one you like best.

If you like to use the mouse, you can paste text back into a document by clicking on the word "Edit" at the top of the Notepad window and then clicking on the "Paste" option. Your text will paste into the point where your cursor is located.

If you would rather use the keyboard to paste your text, you do that by using another control key combination. This time the command is Control-V. Press and hold down the "Ctrl" key and then press the "V" key. Again, your text will paste into the point where your cursor is located.

Congratulations. You've now successfully moved the last paragraph of your letter to the beginning of the letter.

You can use this Cut and Paste method with many paragraphs, or even one word. Simply use the same technique. The only difference would be that you highlight several paragraphs, or just one word, when you go to "Cut."

Copy and Paste

This is similar to Cut and Paste. It's called Copy and Paste and it is very nice if you want to copy something in a document — a word or a paragraph.

It's accomplished exactly as Cut and Paste, except instead of choosing "Cut" from the drop down edit menu (or pressing Ctrl-X) you choose the "Copy" option (or press Ctrl-C).

Let's do this experiment: Try copying the second paragraph of your letter and pasting it at the end of the letter.

First, highlight (select) the second paragraph and then press and hold the Ctrl key and press the "C" key. If you would rather use the mouse, click on the "Edit" option at the top of the Notepad window and click on the "Copy" command.

When you do this it doesn't look like anything happens, but rest assured the computer has copied the selection to its short-term memory, the Clipboard. To get the text out we need to paste it back in. Move the cursor to the end of your letter by pressing the down arrow until you reach the end. (I find it nice to sometimes give myself an extra line of space when pasting; to do this, just hit "Enter" before you paste. You can always remove that extra line later if you want.)

Now, Paste the text you copied into the letter by either clicking on "Edit" and then "Paste" command, or by pressing the Ctrl key and then the "V" key. When you do you'll see the text appear on your screen.

One helpful feature of Cut and Paste, and also Copy and Paste, is that you can paste the text you copied or cut into the same program, or even into another one. This can be very useful. To see how this works, let's open up another copy of Notepad. Remember, to open Notepad you:

1. Click on the "Start" button.

2. Click on "Programs."

3. Click on "Accessories."

4. Click on "Notepad."

You should now have another Notepad window open that is blank. Press "Control-V" or click on "Edit" and then on "Paste". The text you copied and pasted the last time appears on the new Notepad window. Did you notice that you didn't have to copy the text again? The clipboard will usually remember

what you put on it until you copy something else on it.

This can be very handy if you want to use part of a letter in another letter. Cut, Copy and Paste is basically the same in every Windows program you'll ever use.

It also works in word processors and Graphic editing programs, too. You'll use it all the time once you get the hang of it. Practice cutting and pasting until you feel comfortable with it. Try using the mouse and the keyboard, and see which way you like best.

XI.
Spreadsheets

A spreadsheet is like a table of information. One of the most popular spreadsheets ever made is Microsoft's Excel. With it you can create anything from simple to highly complex spreadsheets.

A spreadsheet is a tool for organizing information into rows and columns. The power of a spreadsheet comes from its capacity to sort the information in it by columns, to use formulas for adding up columns, and to produce reports.

A simple example of how you might use a spreadsheet would be to keep a list of your favorite web sites with brief descriptions for each. You could also add information about what's contained on each of the sites. Later you could sort your list any way you wanted.

This example will use Microsoft Excel, but don't worry if you don't have Excel. My example is quite basic and should illustrate just about any spreadsheet program.

When you first start the program you'll have a blank sheet with grid lines dividing it up into little squares.

The first thing you should do is set up the headings you'll use on each column. Let's choose the following: • Name of web site • Web Address • Description.

You'll also need some categories: • Retail • Games • Utilities • Hobby.

All of the little boxes are called cells, and they all have a name too. It's sort of like the old game of Battleship. A1 is the upper left cell. B1 is the next one over across the top. Numbers run down the left side and letters across the top.

First, left click on the first cell (A1) and type in the name for the column, "Name of web site." Notice that the name overlaps into the next cell one over. You can fix this. Put your cursor right between the A and B columns, right over the thin black line that separates them. The cursor will change to a vertical bar with arrows on each side pointing out. Now drag the column over to the right. If you did this correctly the A column will now be much wider than the other columns.

Now start the next column by clicking in B1 and typing in "URL Address" as the name of the column. Drag that column out a bit too. Continue doing this for all the other columns, including the categories. Just put the category columns after the description columns.

Now scroll back to the left so that you can see cell A1. Skip a row and click on the next cell, A3, and start entering the name of the web site, continuing with URL Address, and so on. When you get to the categories, simply type in a '1' if the web site fits into that category, and leave the others blank.

For example, if you were entering the Microsoft web site, you could put a '1' in the retail column because products are sold there. But you can also put 1s in the games and utilities columns too, since those also appear on the Microsoft site.

When you get done inputting your information, you should have something that looks like this.

Typical Spreadsheet

If you wanted to sort the list alphabetically by the name of the web site, you'd click once on the first name in the column, cell A3. Then you'd click on the word "Data" at the top of the window under the title bar, and finally click on "Sort."

A sort window opens, enabling you to sort your list by column in ascending or descending order. If you sort just by column A in ascending order, you'll get an alphabetical list. But you can also sort by two other columns. Why not also sort by column D? This will give you an alphabetical list of retail web sites.

Or, if you just wanted to know what web sites have games, you could sort by column E. The cells with the 1s in them will appear on the top of the list.

This is a highly simplified example. But if you play with it a bit, you should be able to expand on this and make much more complex spreadsheets.

XII.
Simple Bookkeeping

Why not use your computer for some simple bookkeeping? You have all the tools at your fingertips on your computer.

The first thing you need to do is organize. Start by making a folder that is called "taxes" or some other name. Make more folders within the folder. These extra folders will be your categories and/or subcategories. You can make as many of these as you need.

You need to keep a file for each category. It should contain the information on what you spent in that category. Every time you spend money in a particular category, just open the file up and add the information to it.

At the end of the year you can go through your files and print them out. You'll have a detailed list of what you spent on each category. Doing your taxes will be much easier. If you own a small company you could keep folders on each of your employees. You will have all the information at your fingertips when you need it.

If you want to get a bit more advanced, you could make an Excel spreadsheet. You can even design an Excel spreadsheet to do a payroll.

More advanced programs like Microsoft Money or Quicken are available. These specialized programs are designed to keep detailed track of your finances. Either program will also let you manage your personal finances.

If you own a business, Quicken makes a program called QuickBooks. It will manage all your business activities, payroll, print invoices and statements and even keep track of your loans.

One of the big benefits to using your computer for keeping track of all your finances is that you can also buy programs that will compute your taxes.

If you're interested in Quicken, simply go to their website at www.quicken.com for more information and to receive a free trial version. Information on Microsoft Money is available at www.microsoft.com.

Later in the book you'll learn how to use the Internet to find these websites.

Lesson Four

MORE ADVANCED TOPICS

I.

Fun With CDs

A. Making a CD / Burning CDs

If your computer has a CD-ROM writer, you can make your own CDs. The process is called "burning a CD," and it's not that difficult. You'll need a few things before you start, but most computers today have the equipment already installed. If yours doesn't, you can add it to your computer without too much expense.

The first thing you'll need is a CD-ROM writer, or burner as some people call them, and some burning software. Often the software will come packaged with the CD-ROM writer, so check the box to see if you'll need to buy the software separately.

The newest drives will create CDs very quickly. Try to buy the fastest drive you can afford and make sure it'll work with your system. It's not worth getting a really fast drive for an older, slower computer. Although the drive will work, you'll have to slow it down so that the computer can keep up. You can save some money by just purchasing a slower drive. A good speed to go with is 12X, but if you have a newer computer you can try a faster drive. In the end they all make the same CDs, but some drives do it faster than others.

You should also pick up some blank CDs while you're at the store. They are called CD-R, for CD Recordable, and you'll find myriad types and brands. Look for the type that's recommended for your particular CD writer. If you have a 12X writer, make sure the new blank CDs are capable of 12X writing. Not all blank CDs are created equal, and you may have to experiment with a few different brands until you find the best combination for your particular drive. (Faster is ok.)

Once you create a CD with your computer, that CD is final. That means that you can not erase the CD and change it if you make a mistake or want to change it later on. So CD-R is best used for archiving things that you want to keep for a very long time or things you know you'll use often.

If you plan on making music CDs and want the ability to erase and rewrite new music or data onto the CD, then you'll want to pick up some CD-RWs as well. CD-RW stands for CD ReWriteable.

If you have a CD-RW with old backup material that you no longer need, simply erase that material and use the CD for more current backups. CD-RW doesn't burn as fast as regular CDs so it will take a little longer to make a CD-RW than a regular CD with your writer. CD-RW is also more expensive than the regular CD-R and may not work in regular CD players.

B. Installing the CD writer

If you bought your computer and it included a CD writer, then you can skip this section. Also, if you're uncomfortable opening up your computer, have someone else help you install the CD writer.

Installing a CD writer in your computer really isn't as hard as you may think. All you'll need is a screwdriver and about 45 minutes to get the job done. The first thing to do is make sure you look over the instructions that came with your new CD drive so you'll get a general idea about how you'll be doing the installation.

I'll go over the basics in this section, but you'll undoubtedly need to change or adapt some of the techniques mentioned here. That depends on your computer's particular setup.

REMEMBER: Always unplug your computer from the power outlet before you work on it. You can damage it if you touch the wrong element before you detach it from its power source. There's also some possibility of getting damaged yourself.

You can't install something in your computer with the case closed, so remove the screws on the back of the case in order to open it up and gain access to the inside.

One of the worst things you can do to the inside of a computer is to give it a small static electric spark from your fingers as you work on it. Always touch a metal part of the case or frame before you touch any of the computer components inside the computer. Doing this will ground you and get rid of any static electric charge you may have built up in your fingers. Do this even if you don't think there is a risk of static spark. You can not be too safe regarding this.

Take a look at the inside of your computer and locate the CD-ROM drive that's already installed on your system. The drives are usually screwed into a metal box called a drive bay, with the front end of the drive sticking out of your computer. If you have trouble locating your drive, look at the front of your computer and take note of where the front of the CD drive is. Then look directly behind it. Some computers have room to add more than one CD drive. If your computer has such room, it will usually be just below the already installed CD drive.

You may need to remove or punch out a plastic cover so that the empty drive bay is exposed. I've found that the easiest way to do this is to reach inside the computer and push the plastic cover out. But you can also pry it off with a screwdriver or knife if you can't get your hand far enough inside the computer.

If you don't have an empty drive bay, then you'll need to remove the old CD-ROM drive and replace it with your new writer. In any event, you'll see that there are two or three cables/wires attached to the back of the CD drive. The wide flat cable is called a ribbon cable. It may go from the back of the CD directly to the motherboard. Or it may go from the back of the CD drive to another drive, such as a hard disk, before it finally ends up connected to the motherboard. Another cable has four wires, usually a Red, a Yellow and two Black. That's the power cord. Finally, there may be a set of smaller wires going from the back of the CD drive to the sound card in your computer, or they may go directly to the motherboard.

If you're removing the old drive you'll need to unplug these connections so you can attach them to the new CD-Writer. Gently pull on them and they should come loose. Sometimes you may need to pull a fairly hard. If they don't come off, look for a little lever or something that you may need to squeeze or push to release the plug. Once the cables are removed, unscrew the CD-ROM drive and pull it out. Usually it slides out the front of the computer. If not, you'll need to pull it out the back.

If you have enough room to add the new CD-Writer without removing the old CD-ROM drive,then slide the writer into the empty bay and secure it with the screws included with the drive.

Attach the cables to the writer, following the manufacturer's specifications, and close up your computer.

Now turn on the computer and install the CD-Writing software.

C. Burning your first CD

Copying CDs is illegal unless you are making a backup copy for yourself and you already own the original. Don't make copies of music or programs that you don't already own.

For example, it's not legal to borrow your friend's opera CD and make a copy for yourself, but you can make a copy of your own opera CD to use in the car. In fact, making a copy to use in your car is a good idea. If the CD warps or melts you'll still have the original and won't need to buy a new one.

When copying CDs keep this basic rule in mind: If you own it or you bought it, it's probably OK to make a backup copy for yourself. You can, however, use the CD to copy or back up anything that you created, like financial records, pictures, and word processing files.

One of the simplest things to do is make a copy of a complete CD. To get started, insert a blank CD into your CD-Writer and put the music CD you want to copy into the CD-ROM drive. If you only have one drive, start by putting the CD you want to copy into the Writer.

Start the CD copy software and choose the duplicate or copy CD option. The software should prompt you through the process and in a short time you'll have a copy of the music CD.

D. Making a music mix

The fun really starts when you decide to make your own mix of music from the various CDs you have in your collection. Start by deciding what songs you'll want to mix together. Keep in mind that a CD can hold only about 70 or 80 minutes of music.

One of the most popular CD creation programs is called "Easy CD Creator." I'll go over the steps to use this program. However, if you have a different program, you'll likely find that the steps are very similar and that you'll have little difficulty following along.

Whatever CD creation software you use, start the program and choose a new music CD project. The window will probably be divided into two sections. One shows the list of songs on the CD from which you're copying, and the other shows a list of songs you'll be adding to the new CD you're about to create.

You can simply click and drag the songs from the source CD to the new CD you want to create. The songs you click and drag will be added to your new CD when you press the record button. If you're going to be making copies of songs from several different source CDs, then it's a good idea to copy the songs you want on the new CD to your computer's hard disk first. This eliminates the need to swap CDs during the creation process.

Put the source CD in the drive and select the songs you want to copy by clicking on them. Then choose the "convert" or "copy to disk option." In some programs you can simply right click on the track or song you want to copy to your hard disk and choose the convert option.

Create a new folder on your hard disk called "My mix CD," or something like that. Then copy the songs you want into this folder. That way the songs will be easy to find when you're ready to make the final CD.

Pay attention to the area of the save window that lists the type of file you're creating. For best results, select the WAV file (*.WAV) option in the 'Save as type' box. If you don't, you may have difficulties making a CD that will both play and sound good on your CD player.

Another option you may see listed in the "Save as type" box is an MP3 file. These files only play on special MP3 players or computers. Don't choose this option if you're making music CDs for your car or player.

Once you've collected the songs you want on your mix CD, you'll need to actually add them to the new CD project

In the top section of the CD creation software window, find the location to which you saved the songs. This is usually done by clicking on the down arrow next to the Select source files option. Now click on your hard disk and then on the folder you created and saved the songs in.

Once you find the songs, click and drag them to the empty area of the window where the new CD's contents are listed. Click and drag them one by one. They'll be listed in the order you add them. They'll also play in the same order on the final CD.

Usually, near the very bottom of the window is a meter that shows you how much space you have left on the new CD. You can also see how much time you have left on the CD. If you have more time, you can add more songs. If you go over the CD's time limit, you can remove some songs.

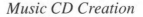

Music CD Creation

Saving Music To Your Hard Disk

Once you're ready, click on the "Record" button or option. A new window will open up giving you control over how the CD will be created. Choose the speed you want to record at and then any other options you may want. As a general rule, always use "Buffer underrun protection" or "Burn proof" protection if you can. When available, these options help you to create a CD without making mistakes that could ruin the CD and require starting over with a new blank CD.

If this is the first time you've created a CD with your drive, then by all means choose the "Test and Record CD" option. As you get more comfortable with your system and you know that everything works, you can switch the option to just "Record CD."

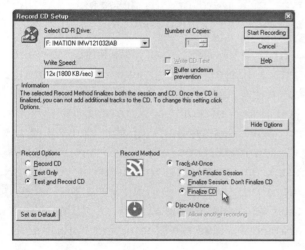

CD Record Options Window

If you do a "Test and Record CD" and the test fails, you'll be able to fix the problem before you start recording the CD. The first thing you'll want to do is slow down the record speed and try the 'Test and Record CD' option again. Do this until the test passes. If you're already at the slowest recording speed and the test still fails, something is wrong with your system and you'll have to call tech support or have someone look at it. A cable may not be plugged in properly or you may need more ram. Chances are it's not

a major problem, but you won't be able to make CDs until you fix it.

In the "Record Method" section of the window, choose the "Track-At-Once" option and then the "Finalize CD" option. This makes the CD playable in CD players. Once you make the CD, you won't be able to change or modify the songs on it unless you're using a CD-RW.

Don't use a CD-RW for playing CDs in your car or other stereo equipment unless you know for sure that your stereo equipment can read CD-RW CDs. Although doing so won't damage your CD player, But you'll save time and minimize frustration by using a regular CD-R. If you do put a CD-RW in your computer and music plays but nothing happens when you put it in your car stereo, your car CD player probably can't read CD-RW and you'll have to make a CD using regular CD-R media.

E. Making a backup of files onto a CD

Making a data CD on a CD that has your computer files rather than music is very much like making a music mix CD. The main difference is that you don't need to copy the files to your computer's hard disk, since they're already there.

Start your CD creation software and select a new Data CD. Then simply find the files you want to add to the blank CD and click and drag them to the new CD. The order in which you add the files to the new CD doesn't matter, since the CD software will alphabetize them for you. When you finish adding files or have filled up the CD, it's time to make the CD. Click on the Record button.

Again, choose the recording speed and select the "Test and Record CD" option if you're new to making CDs. This time you'll want to select the "Track at once" record method and then either the "Finalize session, Don't finalize CD" option or the "Finalize CD" option.

Creating A Data CD

If you've completely filled up the CD or only have a small amount of empty space left, choose the "Finalize CD" option. This option finishes the CD and makes it impossible to add new items to it or change it.

If you've filled up only half of the CD or if you have some space left, then you can choose the "Finalize session, Don't finalize CD" option. This will create the CD but give you the option to add more material to it later on. This is also a bit more advanced and I recommend that you don't use this option until you've created a few CDs and feel comfortable experimenting a bit.

II.

Buying and Selling on eBay.com

Online auctions have recently become one of the most popular ways to buy and sell products over the Internet. What started out as a collector site for PEZ candy dispensers has grown into the largest, most profitable, and best-known online auction site in the world. It's safe to say that you can find just about anything imaginable on eBay — from old toasters to real estate.

If you're just curious, visit *www.eBay.com* and take a look around. From the homepage you can follow the links on the left by clicking on them. The links help you find what you're looking for by breaking down the millions of items for sale on eBay into different categories. If you don't know the category of the item you're seeking, simply type in a word or two describing the item and click the "Find it" button.

After a few seconds you'll be presented with a list of items drawn either from the category you clicked on or from the words you typed in your description. In this list are brief descriptions of the items and the approximate time when the auction ends. Click on the item(s) that interest you to get more information — and even pictures, if they've been provided by the seller. You'll also learn where the bidding currently stands.

At this point you may wish to place a bid of your own. However, before you bid on an item or sell an item, you'll need to register with eBay. Registration is free, quick and simple. All you need is a valid email address or a credit card to validate your identity. A credit card is used only if your e-mail is through an anonymous source such as Hotmail. The credit card information is used only for verification, and no charges are placed on it.

Bidding on an item is easy and fun. Once you find what you're looking for you'll see a box at the bottom of the page letting you know how to bid and what the minimum bid is. Immediately after you make your own bid, eBay will let you know if you are the current high bidder of if someone else has already made a higher bid than yours. You'll also receive later email notification.

It's important to understand that in most cases your bid is a legal contract with the seller. You should not bid on anything unless you can and do intend to purchase it if your bid turns out to be the highest one. This is a very serious matter, so keep this in mind before you actually bid on an item. The safest way to bid is to have a maximum amount that you would pay for an item in mind. Then, don't exceed that amount in your bidding.

If you decide to sell items on eBay, you'll need to register as a seller. Simply click on the 'Sell' link near the top of the homepage and then click on the "New Sellers" link on the following page. You'll need to register your credit card and checking account with eBay in order to be able to sell your item. This is necessary to protect others in the eBay community and to keep people honest.

Although registration to become an eBay seller is free, there are fees — generally small ones — for listing and selling your items. You can view the fee scale at the eBay website. There are usually two fees you pay as a seller: 1) a listing fee and 2) a percentage of the final sale price.

For example, if you sell an item for $20 for which there was a $1 listing fee and a 1% sales fee, your total payment due to eBay for selling the item would be $1.20. The fees used in this example are fictional examples, not actual eBay fees. See the eBay website at www.eBay.com for actual fees.

Once you become a registered seller, you'll need to list your item by choosing a category for it and then typing in a description of it.

Adding one or more photos of the item in your listing usually improves the chances of selling it. There are many ways to do this, but eBay offers an easy-to-use service for doing so. Like the listing itself, the addition of photos requires a small fee. But all you really need are images in a common file format (e.g., jpeg, tiff). eBay takes care of sizing, and the picture automatically appears with your item description every time someone goes to your auction.

Then you sit back and wait for the auction to end. eBay does all the rest, notifying you when the auction has ended and who the high bidder is. Then you contact the winning bidder and arrange for payment and shipping.

III.

Digital Cameras

Using a digital camera can be fun and simple — but only if you take the time to understand how they work. The camera side of a digital camera is pretty straightforward and operates much like a common 35mm camera or even a point-and-shoot type.

Getting the photos into the camera isn't the problem most people have with a digital camera. Getting the pictures from the camera into the computer is usually the tricky part.

The first thing to determine is how your camera connects to your computer. The two most popular methods for connecting digital cameras to computers are serial cable or USB cable, the latter being the easiest and preferred method these days. Most cameras come with the proper cable used to connect camera to computer. If you don't have a cable, check your camera instructions for the type of cable needed for your camera.

Once you connect the cable from your camera to the computer, turn on the camera and install any software that may have come with the camera. Once the camera is set up with the software that came with it, you'll be able to see the pictures that have been stored in it. You'll also be able to copy them to your computer for viewing, editing or saving to disk. Usually you can just click and drag the picture from your camera onto the computer desktop. If this doesn't work, try double clicking the picture in the camera that you want to copy to your computer.

Another much simpler way to get the pictures from your digital camera onto your computer is to use a device called a media reader. These are little boxes that connect to your computer and allow you read the memory card from your digital camera without connecting your camera to the computer. In order to get the correct type of reader for your digital camera, you'll need to know what type of digital media your camera uses. Manufacturers today use a variety of image storage devices. The three major types of digital media are compact flash, smart media, and memory stick. Each type of digital "film" is different, but your digital camera is set up to use only one type. The instructions that came with the camera will tell you what type of media your camera uses. Once you know this information, go to a computer store and ask for a reader that will work with the type of media your camera uses.

When you have the proper media reader hooked up to your computer, you can simply remove the digital storage device from your camera and place it into the reader. From there, double click on the "My Computer" icon on the computer desktop. You'll see a new device in the window. Double click on it and you'll find a folder containing all the images you shot with your camera. Now you have two choices. Either you may click and drag the photos you want to copy to your desktop, or you may double click on the photo file to open it, view its contents, and determine how satisfactory the image is.

Keep in mind that most often the identifying names of the pictures you take are automatically generated by the camera and usually have the date or other numbers in them. So until you look at them you won't know what the pictures are. It's generally recommended that you look at each picture and rename it as you copy it. This may take a little extra time, but later on you'll be able to retrieve the picture you're looking for much more readily.

Editing your photos will require additional software that either came with your camera or that you purchased separately. One of the best programs for editing pictures is made by Adobe and is aptly called Adobe PhotoDeluxe Home Edition. Using the editing and cropping tools in this software program will bring fun into your digital photography experience.

IV.
Cropping Photos

Before you can crop or edit your photos, you'll need to have them copied from your camera to your computer. And, as described above, you'll need some kind of photo editing software.

In addition to Adobe PhotoDeluxe, many other different brands of software are available, so it's possible here to cover only the basics of cropping and editing. You'll have to adjust some of these steps for your particular application.

If you take a look at the screen of your photo editing software, you'll notice some icons or tools that you can click on. One of the most useful is the 'Select" tool. This often looks like a crosshair or perhaps a square made up of dotted lines. When you click or select this tool the pointer on your computer will turn into a crosshair. If you place the pointer over your photo and then click and drag, you'll create a box made up of dotted lines.

When you release the mouse button, the box of dotted lines starts to blink. It looks like its made up of a line of marching ants, all walking around the perimeter of the box you created. This is called a selection.

Now find the tool called crop. By using this, you may delete any part of the picture that's outside the blinking box you've just created. Remaining on your screen will be just the selected section of the picture. The crop command is usually located in a menu. Click on the words across the top of the window. The first word is usually "File." Look under each menu that appears. You may have a menu called "Tools" or perhaps "Commands" or something else that may contain the crop command.

When selecting a section of a picture it's often best to start in the upper-left corner of the area you want to select, and then click and drag down and to the lower-right until you reach the end of your intended selection area.

V.

4-Color Flyers

With your computer, a color printer and a word processor you can create professional looking color flyers, newsletters, posters and stationery. Some programs such as Hallmark Card Studio will even help you to create your own personal greeting cards.

For this example we'll make a flyer you'll use to sell your car. The steps will be general enough so that they should work with just about any word processor. First, you'll need to have a decent photo of your car or whatever you want to sell, so take a picture and get it into your computer as a file. Then, if needed, crop the picture so that the car is the focus of the photograph.

Next, start your word processor program. The most popular ones are Microsoft Word, WordPerfect or Works. Any of them will do the job, but if you have a different word processor it should work fine.

After you have the text you want for the flyer typed in, you can add the picture or pictures of the item you're selling. In most cases this is accomplished from a menu item across the top of the window. Look for either "Insert" or "Tools" and click on it.

In the dropdown list, you should then see an option for inserting a picture or graphic. If you don't find it, look for it in some of the other menus. In Microsoft Word you click on the word 'Insert' then click on the menu option "Picture" and finally on the option "From file…"

Once the picture is in your document, you can "grab" the center of it by moving your mouse around inside it. You'll also be able to click and drag the edges or corners to resize it.

You may wish to add a dash or two of color to your flyer or brochure by using colored text. To change the color of the text you're typing, look in the menus across the top for an option that may be called "Format text" or "Format font," and click on it. Many times this option is under the "Format" menu at the top of the window.

When you click on the format font option, a window opens that allows you to select the size, type and color of the text you are using. After you've made your changes, click on the 'OK' button.

VI.
Scanning Tips

Scanning is more of an art than a science. It takes a bit of fiddling, experimentation, or trial and error to achieve the results you may desire. Keep in mind that you should try to have the best-looking image source you can get. Your scanner doesn't magically fix photos of poor quality. Don't spend endless hours trying to make a bad photo look better. Regardless of your experience with scanning, it's often simply impossible to improve an image that may be blurry, out of focus, too dark, too light, or otherwise weak.

If you're scanning a photo for use on your computer or on a website, or if you intend to email it to somebody, then scan it at a resolution of only 72 dots per inch (dpi). Finally, crop the picture so that it's fairly small. Otherwise the picture will be too large to send over the Internet. An excessively large photo will take a long time for recipients to download, thus leading to the possibility that they won't wait and therefore won't bother to look at the picture you've sent them.

If you're scanning a photo for use in a printed publication such as a flyer or newsletter, you'll need to scan it at a higher resolution — perhaps 150 or 300 dpi. This will give you a better-looking image when it's printed out. Keep in mind, however, that an image with more dots per inch will also take up a lot more storage space on your computer.

VII.
Networking

Networking is a very useful tool that makes it simple to share files between two or more computers. Instead of using a floppy disk, CD, or Zip disk to move programs and files from one computer to another, just click and drag items from one computer to the other using the mouse.

Networking is also handy if, for example, you have a notebook or laptop computer for home or travel use and a standard desktop computer at the office. Networking makes it possible to share programs and files between the two.

Another good use for networking is the sharing of a single Internet connection. If you have a high-speed Internet connection, such as DSL or Cable, then by using a network you can hook up more than one computer, and both can be used to surf the Internet at the same time.

Setting up a network can be a challenging project, but it's not without its rewards. The first thing you'll need in order to network two or more computers are network cards. Network cards plug into your computer, and you'll need one for each computer. The installation is not that difficult. If you buy current network cards that work with the version of Windows you're running on your computer, the installation should be relatively simple.

You'll need to open your computer and install the card in an open slot. If you feel uncomfortable with opening your computer, ask someone else to do it for you. If you do decide to do it yourself, make sure that you unplug the computer before opening it. Also make sure that you touch a metal object that is grounded before you touch the network card or anything else inside your computer. One static electricity spark from your finger to the wrong part inside your computer can damage the machine.

If you plan to hook up only two computers to the network, then you'll need a special network cable called a twisted pair network cable or a null modem cable that you plug into each computer's network card.

If you plan to hook more than two computers together, get a device called a hub, and use regular network cables for plugging your computer into the hub. Each computer gets plugged into the hub with a regular network cable.

The computers don't need to be close to each other either. They can be in different rooms or even on different floors of a building. Of course you'll need network cables long enough to reach from the hub to each computer.

Computer networks once cost thousands of dollars to set up, but today they are quite affordable. Basic network cards can be had for around $25 each. If you need a hub you can usually pick one up for under $40. Network cables are about $1 a foot or less if you buy in larger quantities.

Before buying the parts to set up a network, first check out your computer. Many new computers come with network cards already built in, so you may need to buy only a net-work cable or a hub to set up a home network.

Once you have the hardware and cables all connected, you'll need to program Windows to use the network. Make sure that you've installed any software or drivers that came with your network cards according to the instructions.

On a home network, just like the Internet, each computer must have a unique number, called an IP number, that identifies it for the other computers on the network. This resembles the way in which computers are identified for the Internet. With home networks you should only use certain IP numbers. You don't need to understand all the details; you only need to know the numbers. For your home network I recommend you use these guidelines.

Give each computer on your network a number between 2 and 200. Each computer must have a different number. Write the numbers on a piece of paper so you can refer to them when you set up the network.

Then to get the IP address for each machine put "192.168.0." in front of the number you chose for each computer. For example if I have two computers I want to put on the network I'll identify one computer with the number "2" and the other with "3." That makes each computer's IP address "192.168.0.2" and "192.168.0.3" respectively. Do this for as many computers as you have or want to hook up to your network. The order of the numbers is not important. Feel free to skip around if you want.

The other number you'll need for your home network is called a "Subnet mask" and you can use the following number: "255.255.255.0." Use this number for all the machines on your network.

At this time each computer whose numbers you wrote down on the paper should have two numbers. One number is the IP address and it is "192.168.0.xxx." where xxx is the number you chose. The second number is the Subnet mask, which is "255.255.255.0" for each computer.

The only exception to this rule appears if you are using a special piece of hardware called a router and if the router supports 'DHCP.' If this is the case, then you can plug each of your computers into the router and have it assign the IP addresses and Subnet mask automatically. Routers cost about $150, and they're intended for more advanced users. If you do get a router, follow the directions that came with the it to set up your network.

Now it's time to start each computer and set Windows up for the network.

For Windows XP do the following

1. Click on the "Start" button.

2. Click on the "Control Panel."

3. Click on "Network and Internet Connections."

4. Click on "Setup or change you home or small office network."

5. Follow the steps in the "Network Setup Wizard."

6. Use the IP address and Subnet mask numbers when Windows asks for them.

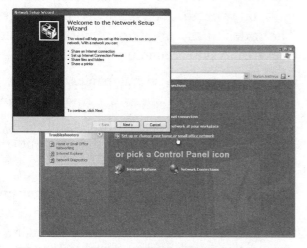

The Network Setup Wizard in Windows XP

For Windows 95, 98 or ME do the following

1. Right click on the "Network Neighborhood" icon on the desktop and select "Properties" from the menu that appears by clicking on it with the left mouse button.

2. Under the "Configuration" tab find your network card and the "TCP/IP" setting. Click on it to select it, and then click on the "Properties" Button.

3. Click on the "IP Address" tab and choose either "Obtain an IP address automatically" or "Specify an IP address." Unless you know that you're using a router or other network device that supports 'DHCP,' you'll need to specify your own IP address. Use "192.168.0.xxx," where xxx is any number between 2 and 200.

4. Set the Subnet mask to 255.255.255.0

5. You can optionally click on the "Default Gateway" tab and enter the IP address of your router or other network gateway, if you're using one. Leave this setting alone if you don't have a router.

6. Click on "OK" and then click on "OK" again to close the configuration windows.

7. You may need to restart your computer.

You'll have to do these steps on each computer that's on the network.

This is a very basic explanation of setting up a network. Networks can become very complex very quickly. There are all kinds of things you need to look at if you have trouble setting up your home network. Some of these are listed below.

• Make sure the cables are plugged in and a light is lit on the back of the network card.

• Check to see if a light is lit on the hub where the network cable is plugged in.

• If you're connecting two computers together, you'll need a special cable. Make sure you have the special cable or use a hub and two cables to connect the computers.

• Make sure that your network card is installed properly and that any drivers that came with it are installed and working.

If all else falls, you may be in just a bit over your head. Don't panic. Everyone who has ever set up a computer network has felt this way. See if you can get help from someone at a local computer store, or have a friend look your system over. Nine times out of ten it's just a small problem causing the networking problem.

Lesson Five

THE INTERNET

The United States Government started the Internet in the 1960s as a system of communication between universities and research facilities. At the time it wasn't called the Internet, and it worked very slowly.

As the universities experimented with it, they realized that it was becoming an important tool for them. The Internet continued to evolve over the next couple of decades—almost unnoticed by the general public.

By the late 1980s the Internet had become generally available, but most people still looked upon it as a waste of time. The government and universities were still using it, however, and new ways of viewing the Internet were developing.

It was around this time that the first real browser (a program used to view the Internet) became available. This changed everything. Now, with the use of these new browsers, the Internet was easier to use and began to look better to everyone.

Then, almost overnight, more and more people began talking about the Internet. An increasing amount of information was being put on-line, and some companies were even starting to sell products on the Internet.

Stories began circulating about people who had become instant millionaires by doing some very simple and creative things with the Internet. Such stories fueled a frenzy that's still burning today. People flocked to the Internet just to see what all the fuss was about—and also perhaps to stake their claim for a million or two.

Today the experiment is over. The Internet has grown into something no one could have predicted a few years ago. It has become a new communications medium that will someday connect every single human on this planet to everyone else.

If you want to see the sun rise in Spain, you can. From your home computer, you can tap into hundreds of cameras posted all over the planet. You can get the weather for any location on Earth. And, if you want the inside scoop on what's going on in China, why not talk to someone who lives there? You can do all these things today, and it'll cost you only a few dollars a month.

All kinds of people are on the Internet. Because it's not owned by anyone or by any one country, there are no real rules for using it. Don't let this scare you, though. If you use just an ounce of common sense, you'll be able to avoid the parts of the Internet you don't want to see, and to stay in the parts that interest you. Treat the Internet just as you treat the people and places in your real life. If you bump into someone or something you don't like, just leave with a click or two of your mouse.

As for potential problems with children and the Internet, consider this. You wouldn't let your kids play downtown unsupervised, would you? The Internet is like an immense downtown containing elements from all walks of life. Exercise the same caution with the Internet as you would if your children were going to play downtown. Maintain the needed control over their contact with people and places — in real life and in cyber life.

The Internet has become so vast that it's often spoken of as another place. In a way it is. You can go shopping, travel, or have a family reunion on it. You can also research the inner workings of an F-15 fighter jet. It's all at your fingertips, no further away than your computer screen. And most of it is offered free of charge.

The Internet isn't difficult to use. Millions use it all the time. Some are young or naive, others are sophisticated and highly educated adults, and the rest are somewhere in between. Using this new communications medium is a lot like changing the channels on your television. In fact, there are televisions that can now browse the Internet.

The hardest part about using the Internet is finding what you want in a crowded sea that holds billions of topics. Sometimes you really can feel as though you're looking for the proverbial needle in a haystack.

Relax and read on. In no time you'll be surfing the Internet and having a ball.

I.
Words You Should Know

Just like the computer, the Internet has its own little buzz words. Look this list over and learn what the terms mean. Some of them are rather abstract, but a complete and full understanding of every term in this list isn't necessary for you to enjoy the Internet. I'm providing this list of terms so you won't feel completely lost when you hear someone throwing them around in conversation.

ADSL: This is a fancy name for a new type of Internet connection. This new system uses the phone lines that are already in your home and can provide much faster speeds of connection. That means you can get more graphics faster when you're on the Internet. The down side is that it doesn't work everywhere yet.

Bookmark: This is like a placeholder for the Internet. You can use bookmarks to go quickly to a favorite web page without having to type in the web page address.

Call waiting: Many people with a single phone line use this feature so that when they're talking on the phone they'll know if someone else is trying to call them. This feature doesn't work with computers. Turn it off when you're using your computer for the Internet.

Connect: This means to call up the Internet. When two or more computers are on the Internet together at the same time, they are connected.

Cable Modem: A high speed modem connection used with your cable TV provider. Very fast, but may slow down if many people in your neighborhood their cable modem at the same time. As good or better than ADSL.

Dial-Up: This is a part of Windows that lets your computer "Dial-Up" the Internet just like you dial up a friend.

Download: This means getting a file or a program from the Internet. When you check your e-mail, you're downloading it to your computer.

E-commerce: Buying things over the Internet.

E-mail: This is like regular mail that you can send to friends and businesses, but it's electronic. Hence the "e." E-mail can be sent to anyone with an e-mail address. Most of the time the mail gets to the recipient in a few minutes. E-mail is also free.

Hyperlink: This is a special spot on a web page that you can click on. Doing so will whisk you to another place on the Internet.

Internet: The name used to describe all the computers in the world that are hooked up into one big network.

ISDN: A special kind of phone line that you need to have the phone company bring into your home. It's more expensive than regular phone lines, but it provides faster connection speeds.

ISP: Internet Service Provider. This is the company that you pay every month for enabling you to get onto the Internet with your computer.

Link: Another name for a hyperlink. When you click on a link, it'll take you to a different place on the Internet.

Login: Getting on the Internet requires that you have an account. When you access your account and get on the Internet, you've logged in.

Logon: See Login.

Modem: This is the part of your computer that the phone line plugs into.

News group: Groups on the Internet where users talk about different subjects. There are news groups for just about every subject imaginable.

Password: A secret combination of letters or numbers that you login with and use to gain access to your Internet account.

Protocol: A computer language that your computer uses to talk with other computers on the Internet. If your computer doesn't have the proper protocol set up, it won't work on the Internet. Similarly, if you speak only English but want to talk to someone who speaks only French, you can't do it easily because you both use different protocols.

Pulse dialing: An older telephone system that used a series of clicks to dial numbers. Old phones with turning dials on them are pulse phones.

TCP/IP: This is the protocol of the Internet. Your computer must have this protocol (language) set up or you won't be able to use the Internet.

Tone dialing: A newer type of phone system that dials numbers by playing beeping sounds. Tone dialing phones have buttons on them to dial the numbers.

The Web: Another name for the World Wide Web or the Internet.

URL: Universal Resource Link. A fancy name for "Internet address." You type a URL into a browser in order to get to a web page. This is known as the web address.

Username: This is the name that your ISP (Internet Service Provider) gives you so you can access your Internet account and login.

World Wide Web: Another name for the web or Internet.

Exercise # 1
Complete the following

1. You can use these to quickly go to a web page you like without having to type in the web page address. They are _____ _____.

2. Groups on the Internet where users talk about different subjects are _____.

3. A newer type of phone system that dials numbers by playing beeping sounds is _____.

4. When you call up the Internet you _____ _____.

5. A special kind of telephone line that the phone company brings into your home. It is more expensive than a regular telephone line, but it gives you faster connection speeds. It's called _____.

6. Getting a file or a program from the Internet and putting it on your computer is called _____ _____.

7. Many people with a single telephone line use this feature so that when they are on the phone talking to someone they will know if someone else tries to call them. It's called _____ _____.

8. Buying or selling things over the Internet is called _____.

9. Another name for a hyperlink is _____.

10. The part of your computer that the telephone line plugs into is the _____.

11. A special spot on a web page that you can click on to go to another place on the Internet is called a _____.

12. The name used to describe all the computers in the world that are hooked up into one big network is _____.

13. The company that you pay every month so that you can use your computer to get onto the Internet is called your _____.

14. The secret combination of letters or numbers that you use to gain access to your Internet account and login is your _____.

15. Getting on the Internet with a username and password is called _____.

16. A fancy name for a new type of Internet connection. This new system uses the phone lines that are already in your home. It is called _____ _____.

17. An older telephone system that uses a series of clicks to dial numbers is _____.

18. The part of Windows that lets your computer connect to the Internet is _____ _____.

19. The protocol of the Internet is _____.

20. Like regular mail that you can send to friends and businesses but it is free. This is _____.

21. A big fancy name for an Internet address is _____.

22. The name that your ISP (Internet Service Provider) gives you so that you can access your Internet account and Login is _____.

II.
Modems

A modem is the device your computer uses to call the Internet. Most modems have two phone plugs in back. One connects with the phone line and the other with your phone. This way you can still use your phone when your computer isn't using the line.

— Modem

Modems come in many styles and speeds. Most modems are built into your computer and have the plugs coming out the back of the computer. But some are separate boxes that plug into the back of the computer with a cable. No matter which style you have, they both operate essentially the same.

Modem speed is usually given in numbers, such as 28.8K or just 28.8 or 33.6. You don't need to know what the numbers really mean. The bigger the number the faster the modem. You should make sure you have the fastest modem you can afford. The speed really makes a difference.

Today the fastest modems around are 56.6K modems, sometimes referred to as X2 modems. As a general rule, don't get anything less than a 33.6K modem. 28.8K is okay if you really can't find or afford anything faster.

If you have money to spare, you can buy one of the faster, more expensive modems, like ISDN, but they require that a new phone line be brought into your home. This isn't recommended for the average Internet user.

For those readers who really want to know what the modem numbers mean, read on. Otherwise, you can skip to the next section.

The numbers are expressed in bits per second. A bit is a small packet of information, like the letters in our language. Consider this. To send the word "the," you'd need three letters, obviously.

To measure how fast you communicate that word to someone else, you might use letters per second as your unit of measurement. In the case of a modem, the unit of measurement is bits per second. The 'K' at the end tells you to multiply the number by 1,000. This means that a 28.8K modem is really a 28,800 bits per second modem.

That explains why the bigger the number the faster the modem.

A. Setting up your modem

If you're putting a new modem in your computer, carefully follow the instructions given by the manufacturer. The following instructions are only basic guidelines.

To check if your modem is set up properly, open the control panel and double click on the "Modems" icon.

For Windows XP use the following steps

1. Click on the "Start" button and then on "Control Panel."

2. Click on "Printers and Other Hardware."

3. Click on "Phone and Modem Options."

4. Enter your location information and telephone area code if you are asked for it. Then click on the "Modem" tab at the top of the window.

For all other Windows versions

1. Click on the "Start" button.

2. Put the pointer over "Settings" and hold it there for a second.

3. Click on the "Control Panel" option that pops up.

4. Find the "Modems" icon and double click on it.

You should now be looking at the "Modem Properties" window. At the top are two tabs, "General" and "Diagnostics." Below that you should see an info box that has a list of modems installed on your computer. At the bottom you should see a button that says "Dialing Properties."

Modem Properties Window

Your modem should appear in the list. If you don't see it, you can try to add it by clicking on the "Add..." button. When you do this, Windows will ask if you want it to try detecting your modem automatically. This is recommended for new users. Make sure that you've got handy any disks or CDs that may have come with your modem. Windows may ask you for them.

If you do see your modem listed, check out some of the properties you can set. Click once on your modem in the list so that it's highlighted. Then click on the "Properties" button.

A new window of properties will pop up. You can adjust the speaker volume for your modem here. Usually, when your modem starts to dial out to the Internet, you'll hear it for awhile. This way you can monitor what the modem is doing. If you need to, though, you can turn the sound down or off from this window.

Now click on the "Connection" tab on your modem's properties window. You'll be leaving most of these settings alone. But there are a few things you can safely play with. In the middle of this screen is the "Call preferences" section. You'll see some check boxes next to the options.

It's usually a good idea to have all these options checked, but you don't have to have them checked for your modem to work. By checking the "Wait for dial tone before dialing" option, you can have your modem pick up the phone and listen for the dial tone. If you turn this off, your modem will dial out a bit faster. But if you or someone else is on the line, the modem will just dial out over the top of the conversation.

The second option, "Cancel the call if not connected within..." is also a good one to have checked. That way your computer won't dial a number and just wait forever for someone to answer. A good time to set is 60 seconds.

The third option, "Disconnect a call if idle for more than..." will make the computer hang up automatically if you forget to hang up or if you stop using the modem for a specified amount of time. A good setting for this is 30 minutes.

Here's a handy tip if you use tone dialing. (If your phone makes beeping sounds when you dial out, you're using tone dialing.)

Click on the "Advanced" button at the bottom of this screen. When you do, a new window will open up called "Advanced Connection Settings." At the bottom of this window you'll see a section called "Extra settings" and an input box below it. Enter "S11=50" into the input box. Then click on the "OK" button. Click again on the "OK" button, and this should bring you back to the "Modem Properties" window.

Advanced Connection Settings Window

The setting you just made will make the modem dial the Internet much faster. Give it a try. If for some reason it doesn't seem to be working with your phone system, you can go back and change the number. Make it larger. Try "S11=70" next. Or, if it still doesn't seem to work, just take the line out altogether by backspacing over it until it disappears.

Now click on the "Dialing Properties" button toward the bottom of the window. This is the window where you tell your computer how to dial out. You really don't have to enter any of the information here to make your computer work properly. But you do need to give some attention to two very important settings.

The first setting you need to verify is the "To disable call waiting, dial:" option. If you have call waiting, you must put a check mark next to this box. Next you will

have to tell the computer how to turn off call waiting by using the option in the list box just to the right of this option. Click on the down arrow. From the list choose the proper way to turn off call waiting.

You may have to call your phone company for this information. Phone systems can vary, so here's a tip to keep in mind.

Ordinarily, to turn off call waiting you dial a code and then wait for a dial tone. Let's pretend that you have to dial "70" and then wait for a dial tone before dialing your number "555-1212."

If you find that your computer is dialing the first part ("70") but is then starting to dial the phone number ("555-1212") before the dial tone, you can fix this in the following way.

Notice, one of the options for turning off call waiting is "70,,". But why the commas? A comma tells the computer to wait a little bit. So what this is telling the computer is to dial seven, then zero, then to wait a bit, then wait a bit more, and then dial the number. If your computer is starting to dial the phone number before the dial tone, it's not waiting long enough. So just add an extra comma at the end of the "70,," making it "70,,," and try that. You can add as many commas as you need.

Later, when you try dialing out, if you find that this is your problem, then come back to this section and fix it.

The second option you need to make sure of is the "Dial using:" section. Here you have two choices — tone dial or pulse dial. If you don't know what type of phone system you have, try tone dial. If the modem doesn't work, try pulse dial.

If all else fails, call your phone company and ask them what type of service you have in your home.

When you're finished checking these settings, just click on the "Close" button and the window will close, keeping your settings.

B. Dial-up networks

In the last section you made sure that your modem was set up properly. In this section you'll learn how to use your home telephone line to link your computer to the Internet. We need to tell the computer how to use the phone to dial the Internet.

Before starting this, you'll need a few things, the first being an account with an Internet provider. You can get one if you don't already have one by looking in the yellow pages under Internet or computer, or by talking to friends who are already on-line.

Your Internet provider should give you some vital information that you'll need to finish this section. You should have the computer dial-up number, a user name, and a password. Also, it's wise to have the provider's voice number in case you need to call them for anything. Write all this down and have it handy.

The computer uses a program called "Dial-Up Connection" to make the phone call. This stores the information you give it, such as phone number, user name, and password. Once it's set up, you'll be able to dial the Internet and connect to it with just one double click.

Make sure that you've correctly set up your modem. If you're unsure or still need to set it up, go to the previous section and follow the directions.

Note: For Windows XP Users

Windows XP has greatly reduced the number of steps needed to set your computer up to use the Internet. The best way to get your computer set up to dial your Internet Service Provider is to use the "New Connection Wizard" and follow the on-screen steps.

To start the wizard, follow these steps.

1. Click on the "Start" button and then on the "Control Panel"

2. Click "Network and Internet Connections"

3. Click "Set up or Change Your Internet Connection."

4. Click the "Set up" button near the top of the window and follow the on-screen instructions.

If you have any problems getting your dial-up connection to call your ISP and log you on, double check your settings and make sure that your user name and password are typed in correctly. Capitalization does count with some Internet providers, so be sure to type in the information exactly as it was given to you.

If you still can't get your computer to connect to your Internet provider, call them. They may have to change some settings on their system, or they may need you to make special settings on your computer. They should be happy to help you. After all, that's what you're paying them for.

**Windows XP Users continue with
III. Browsers**

For All Other Windows Users

Following are the steps for setting up the "Dial-Up" connection. If at anytime you make a mistake, just click on "Cancel," close all open windows, and start over on step one.

1. Close all programs. You should see only your desktop. If there are any open windows close them.

2. Find the "My Computer" icon and double click on it.

3. In the window that opens, double click on the "Dial-Up Networking" folder.

106

4. On some computers a "Dial-Up Net-working" connection wizard will open automatically. If it does, just click on "Next." If not, find the program called "Make New Connection" in the "Dial-Up Networking" window and double click on it.

5. The first thing you want to do now is enter a name for the connection. If you want, you can keep the name your computer gave it, which is most likely "My Connection."

6. If your modem was properly set up, you should see it in the next box. If you don't see your modem, click on the down arrow at the end of the box and select it from the list that appears. If your modem isn't in the list, click "Cancel." Close all open windows and return to the modem setup section. (Refer to Section A of Modems.)

7. If you've typed in your name and if your modem is selected in the box, you can now click on "Next" at the bottom of the window.

8. Enter the phone number that your Internet Service Provider (ISP) gave you. Type the number into the box provided for the phone number.

9. Click "Next."

10. Windows now will give you a verification screen and allow you to check your settings. Click "Finish."

You've just created a dial-up account. Now you need to tweak it a bit. Right click on the new "Dial-Up Network" program you just created. Left click on the word "Properties" in the box that opens. Then make the following changes.

- No check mark next to "Log On To Network."

- Check mark next to "Enable Software Compression."

- No check mark next to "Require Encrypted Password."

Under the "Allowed Network Protocol" section of the window, make the following changes.

- No check mark next to "NetBEUI."

- No check mark next to "IPX/SPX Compatible."

- Check mark next to "TCP/IP."

Click on "OK." You're done. The only thing you may want to do is make a shortcut on your desktop for an easy call-up procedure. Right click on the "Dial-Up Network" program and hold the mouse button down. Drag the program out onto a blank area of your desktop and release the right mouse button.

Windows will now ask if you want to create a shortcut here. Put the cursor over the words "Create shortcut here" and left click. You now have a shortcut on the desktop. Merely double clicking on the shortcut will make your computer call the Internet.

Try it now and Windows will open a new window containing two empty boxes for "User Name" and "Password." There may be some information in them. If it's not correct, click on a box and change the information so that it has your "User Name" in the appropriate box. Then click on the password box and type in your new password.

Note: When you type in your password you won't be able to see it. All you will see is a line of asterisks (****) for the letters you type in. Be careful not to make any mistakes when entering the password. If you do, just backspace all the way and start over again.

Since you probably don't want to type in your password every single time you log on to the Internet, you should put a check mark in the box next to "Remember my password" by clicking on the box.

If other people will be using your computer and you don't want them to be able to get onto the Internet with your computer, leave this box unchecked. Then each time you double click on the Internet connection it will ask you for your password. Anybody using your computer would have to ask you for your password to use your Internet account.

After you've entered your name and password and decided whether or not to check the password option, click on the "Connect" button. Your computer will now start to dial up your ISP and connect you to the Internet.

Once the computer connects, it'll give you a connection window. Click on "OK" and a small telephone will appear on your task bar by the clock. To hang up the phone, put the cursor on top of the small telephone and right click on it. Then put the cursor over the word "Disconnect" and left click. Your computer will hang up.

If you have any problems getting your dial-up connection to call your ISP and log you on, double check your settings and make sure that your user name and password are typed in correctly. Capitalization does count with some Internet providers, so be sure to type in the information exactly as it was given to you.

If you still can't get your computer to connect to your Internet provider, call them. They may have to change some settings on their system, or they may need you to make special settings on your computer. They should be happy to help you. After all, that's what you're paying them for.

III.

Browsers

A browser is a special program that you use to see the Internet. At this time there are two main browsers available, Netscape Communicator and Internet Explorer. They're both pretty much the same thing, and it really doesn't matter which one you use. Since there are a few small differences between them, I'll discuss the setup for each one separately. If you need to, just skip ahead to the section that describes the browser you're using.

A. Netscape Communicator™

Netscape is the older of the two browsers described in this book. If you've been on the Internet for a few years, you're surely familiar with this program. Netscape comes with a mail program also.

If you don't have a current version of Netscape, you can always get it by visiting Netscape's web site at www.netscape.com and looking for a download option. It's usually at the very top, but the web site changes often and things get moved around.

Netscape is a large program, so even if you have a fast modem, it'll take a long time to download it. If you don't want to waste the time doing that, you can order it on CD-ROM.

Once you get Netscape and install it, you'll have to give it certain information before it'll be able to get and send your e-mail. You'll have to get this information from your ISP. Call up your Internet Service Provider and ask them for the information in the following list. Tell them you plan on using it to set up Netscape to get your mail and news.

1. Your e-mail address:

_____

2. Your incoming mail server name:

_____

3. Incoming mail server type:

_____

4. Your outgoing mail server name:

_____

5. Your news server name:

_____

6. Your mail server user name:

_____

If you're installing Netscape for the first time, just follow the on-screen directions and answer the questions. If Netscape is already on your computer, run the program now by double clicking on it.

If you're not sure whether Netscape is on your system, you can look through the programs listed under the "Start" button on your task bar. If Netscape is already installed on your computer, you should see it listed here.

Now click on the word "Edit" in the Netscape window at the top right under the title bar. A new window will open up. This is where you can put the information you got from your ISP.

window, starting with "File" and going across, you'll see a group of settings called "Mail and News" preferences. This is where you go to enter the information.

You now see a list of options on the left and the settings on the right side of this window. Put the cursor on top of the words "Mail & Newsgroups" and double click. When you do this a list of other options should appear. Click once on the "Identity" option and check the setting on the right side.

If you need to, enter your name and e-mail address in this window. Then click on the "Mail Servers" option on the left side of this window.

Take a look at the "Incoming Mail Servers" box. If the mail server your ISP gave you is not listed, click on the "Add…" button and enter the information.

Now look at the "Outgoing Mail Server" box below. If it doesn't list the information your ISP gave you, put it in. Below that is the box for "Outgoing mail server user name." This is the name you got from your ISP, so enter it as well.

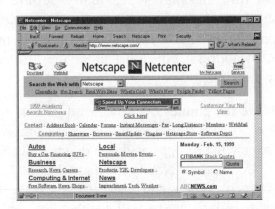

Netscape Netcenter™

Note: If you're using an older version of Netscape, you can still use the information you got from your ISP to set it up. If you look through the menus at the top of the Netscape

Preferences

Click once on the "Newsgroup Server" option in the left side of the window. Look at the server that's listed in the box on the right side of the window. If it's not the same as the one your ISP gave you, click on the "Add…" button and put in the information you got from your ISP.

Click on the "OK" button at the bottom. You can now check your settings to see if they're correct. Close all programs and windows. Then double click on the "Dial-Up Connection" you made in the last section and log onto the Internet.

Once your computer tells you that it's connected to the Internet, double click on the Netscape icon or run it from the "Start" button.

Netscape E-mail

Now click on the "Communicator" option in the Netscape window. Then click on the word "Messenger." A new window will open up. This is the "Mail" window. Next, click on the "Get Msg" button at the top of this window. If everything has been set up properly, you should get your e-mail. Remember that if you're a new user you may not have any mail, so it may look like it's not working.

Get the e-mail address of one of your friends and click on the "New Msg" button at the top of the Netscape window. A new window called "Composition" will open. The figure below gives a description of this window and its parts.

Composition

Click on the top line called "To:" and enter your friend's e-mail address. Then click on the "Subject:" line and type in the subject of this e-mail. Now click in the big box at the bottom. This is where you type the letter itself. When you finish the letter, you can click on the "Spelling" button at the top of this window to check your spelling.

When you're satisfied with everything, click on the "Send" button at the top left of the window and your message will be sent. If you get any errors, check your settings. If you can't find anything wrong, call your ISP and explain that you're having problems sending your mail. They may have to make some changes on their end or have you make special settings on your computer.

Take a closer look at the "Composition" window. Click on the "New Msg" button if you need to.

Now type in your friend's e-mail address again, but this time when you're done press the "Enter" key on your keyboard. When you do this another "To:" box appears below your friend's e-mail address. You can send this message to as many people as you want to just by pressing "Enter" and typing in another e-mail address. Enter your e-mail address, but don't press the "Enter" key this time.

Move the pointer over the word "To" at the left of your e-mail address and click once on it. A new list of options drops down. Click on the "Cc" option. Now your name has a "Cc" next to it. When you send this message to your friend, he or she will see that you sent a copy of this e-mail to yourself.

Netscape E-mail Attachments

What if you wanted to send your friend a picture, or for that matter any other file on your computer? To do this you need to attach the file to your e-mail. This may sound hard but it isn't. Across the top of the composition window, right below the menu options, is a group of buttons called "Send," "Quote," "Address," "Attach: ..." Click on the "Attach:" button.

When you click on "Attach," you can select to attach a file or a web page. Don't worry about the other option(s). You need to know only how to attach a file or a web page.

Click on "File" and a window will open up that allows you to search your hard disk in order to find the file you want to attach. You should know where that file is, but if you don't, you'll have to look for it by using the "Find" option described earlier. If you've forgotten some things about files and about how and where they get put, go back and review.

When you find the file you want to attach, click on it to highlight it, and then click on the "Open" button. You'll see the file in the "List of attachments" box in the "Composition" window. You can click on the "Attach" button again and attach another file if you want.

You can attach any type of file you want to — a picture, a word processor document, or anything else you have on your computer. You should try to keep it small because it'll take a long time to send the message if you attach a big file. Your friend might not appreciate receiving a message that takes an hour to download.

Now click on the "Attach" button again. This time select "Web page." A new window will open up asking you to specify the web page (URL). Type the web page address in this box and click on the "OK" button. Netscape will then attach the web page to your e-mail.

Normally, you'd then type in a message and press the "Send" button to send the e-mail. But this time click on the "Close"

gadget in the upper right corner of the composition window.

Netscape may warn you that the message has not been sent and ask you if you want to save the message. Click the "No" button.

If you ever start making a letter and then decide you don't want to send it you can always click on the close gadget and answer "No" to the save question. When you do this, the message is gone forever.

When you do get a message from a friend, you can read it by clicking on it. Sometimes it's best to maximize this window so that you can see more of the message on the screen. When you're done reading your friend's message, you can quickly send a response letter by clicking on the "Reply" button. When you do this, Netscape automatically puts your friend's e-mail address in for you and also copies the original message into the window. Type in the response to your friend's message, and press "Send" when you're done.

After you've finished with your friend's e-mail, you can delete it from your list by selecting the message and pressing the "Delete" key on your keyboard. There are other ways you can delete a message too. You can click and drag it over the trash can in the Netscape mail window. Or you can select the message, click on the "Edit" menu, and select the "Delete" option.

Just as Windows lets you get into the recycle bin, Netscape allows you to go into the trash folder and look for any messages. After awhile, the trash folder in Netscape will start to fill up. About once a month or so you should go into this folder and delete all the old messages.

To do this you need to click once on the trash folder and then click once on a message that's in the trash folder. Then follow these steps.

1. Click on the "Edit" menu at the top of the window.

2. Click on the "Select" option and then on the "All messages" option.

3. Press the "Delete" key on your keyboard.

Newsgroups

In the mail window you should see your news server listed at the bottom below the trash can on the left side of the window.

Looking For Newsgroups

Click on it once to highlight it. Now right click on it and select "Subscribe to news groups." This is a free service provided by the ISP. After a while you'll see the window start to fill up with a big list of newsgroups.

You can browse through this list until you find a news group you'd like to subscribe to. When you do find such a group, you can subscribe by clicking on the "Subscribe" column next to the name of the newsgroup.

Selecting A Newsgroup

When you're done, click on the "OK" button. Your messenger window should now have your regular inbox and trash, but you should also see a new listing under your news server. You should see the news group(s) you subscribed to. Click on one of the news groups and you'll see the messages in it. You can then read, delete, or respond to any of the messages you see in the news groups.

If at anytime you want to stop reading a newsgroup, just right click on the newsgroup and then click on "Remove newsgroup." It will be removed from your computer.

B. Internet Explorer™

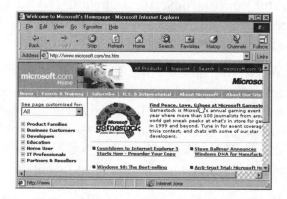

Microsoft Internet Explorer

Most likely this browser is already installed on your computer. It's packaged with Windows, and because of that many people use it.

In order to set this browser up, you should have the following information, which you'll have to get from your ISP. The following list is a good guide for telling them what you need when you call them for the information. Tell them you're going to use it to set up Internet Explorer to get your mail and news.

1. Your e-mail address:
   _____

2. Your incoming mail server name:
   _____

3. Incoming mail server type:
   _____

4. Your outgoing mail server name:

_____

5. Your news server name:

_____

6. Your mail server user name:

_____

If you're installing Internet Explorer for the first time, just follow the on-screen directions and answer the questions. If Internet Explorer is already on your computer, run the program now by double clicking on it.

Click on "Tools" and then on "Internet Options." This brings up a configuration window. You will see a group of tabs across the top, but you need to be concerned with only three right now.

*   General
*   Connection
*   Programs

In "General" you can set the address of a page that will automatically come up each time you run Internet Explorer. If you don't have an Internet address to put in this box, just leave it alone. Later, when you do know what page you want to have Internet Explorer start with, you can come back and change it.

Now click on the "Connection" tab. Make sure that "Connect to the Internet using a modem" is selected by clicking on the circle just to the left of it. Then make sure there isn't a check mark in the box next to "Access the Internet using a proxy server." Then click on the "Settings" button.

At the top of the "Dial-Up Settings" window, make sure that the option "Use the following Dial-Up Networking connection" is set to use the dial-up connection you created in the previous section. If your dial-up is not listed in the box, click on the down arrow and select it from the list. If you don't see your dial-up in the list, click on the "Add" button and make one now. When you're done, click on "OK."

After you've done the above, click on the "Programs" tab at the top of the window. The "Mail" and the "News" settings should both be set to Outlook Express. If either of them isn't set, right click on the down arrow and select it from the list.

To finish the settings, click on the "OK" button. All that remains is to set up the mail settings. Click on the word "Go" at the top of the Internet Explorer window, and then click on "Mail." If you get the "Internet Connection Wizard" window, select "Create a new Internet Mail account" and follow the on-screen instruction.

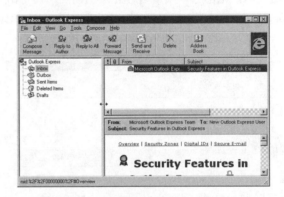

Outlook Express

When the "Inbox – Outlook Express" window opens, click on the word "Tools" near the top of the window, and then click on "Accounts." You should now be looking at the "Internet Accounts" window. There are some tabs at the top of this window. Click on the "Mail" tab. If anything is listed in this window, remove it. Then click on the "Add" button and answer the questions using the information you got from your ISP.

When you're done setting up your mail account, click on the "News" tab at the top. If anything is in this window, remove it. Then click on the "Add" button and enter the info you got from your ISP. When you're done, click on the "Close" button in the lower right corner of the window.

Internet Explorer E-mail

Now click on the "Send and Receive" button near the top of the Outlook Express window. Your computer should get your mail as well as send anything you've typed. This is how you get your mail.

To send a message, just click on the "Compose Message" button and a new window will open up. Type the message here. But first, at the "To" field, enter your friend's e-mail address. If you also want to send a copy of the message, you can enter another e-mail address in the "Cc" box. Then type in a subject in the "Subject" box. Now you can start typing your letter. Just click inside the large area in the bottom half of the window and start typing.

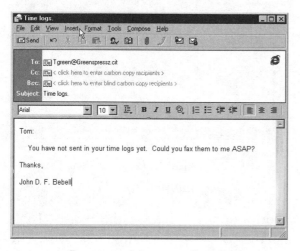

Compose Message Screen

Internet Explorer E-mail Attachments

If you want to attach a file to your e-mail, such as a photo, just click on the word "Insert" at the top of the window, and then on "File attachment." This opens a new window called "Insert Attachment." Browse through your hard disk until you find the file you want to attach. Click once on that file to select it and then click on the "Attach" button. When you do this, the window disappears and the e-mail message window will come back to the top. At the very bottom of the window you should

see the attached file. When you send the e-mail to your friend, he or she will receive the photo too.

When you're done reading an e-mail, you can delete it by clicking the "Delete" button near the top of the "Inbox" window. When you do, it puts the message in the "Deleted Items" folder. If this folder starts to fill up, you can empty it by clicking on it in the list on the left of the window. Then click on one of the deleted messages on the right of the window. Now click on the word "Edit" at the top of the window and select all of the deleted messages by clicking on "Select All." All of the messages should be highlighted now. Finally, to get rid of them click again on the word "Edit," and then click on the "Delete" option. Now all of your messages will be gone.

To read newsgroups, click on the word "Go" and then on "News." This opens the news window. If a message here tells you that you're not a current subscriber to any newsgroups, you'll be asked if you'd like to view a list of available newsgroups. Assuming you'd like to see such a list, click on "Yes." You should now see a list of all the newsgroups that are available to you. It may take a few minutes to get the entire list, so just sit back and wait for it.

After the list loads, type in a word at the top and your computer will automatically sort the list for you. When you find a newsgroup you want to read, click on the "Subscribe" button. If you want to unsubscribe from it, click on the "Unsubscribe" button. When you're done, click on the "Go to" button and the window will close. At the left of the Outlook Express window, you'll see a list of the newsgroups you subscribed to. Click on one of them to start reading the messages in it.

If at anytime you want to subscribe to a newsgroup or unsubscribe from one, just click on the "News groups" button near the top of the window.

C. Browser basics

No matter which browser you use, they share many similarities in operation. Take a look at Figures B-1 and B-2 and this should become obvious.

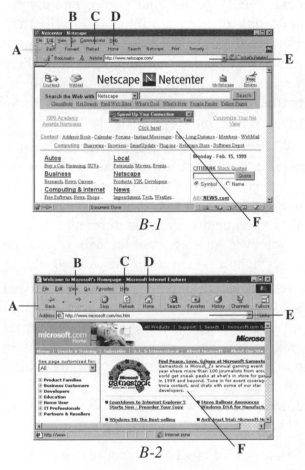

B-1

B-2

The similar buttons and features are:

A. Back button.

B. Forward button.

C. Reload and Refresh buttons.

D. Home button.

E. Location and Address box.

F. Browser window.

Log onto the Internet at this time and launch your browser. Maximize the browser so that it's as large as it can be. Take a look at

Figures B-1 and B-2 and find these buttons on your browser.

You'll see that the browser is broken up into two main parts — the buttons at the top of the window and a browser window at the bottom. The browser window is large and takes up most of the screen. That's where web pages are displayed. The buttons are the controls you'll use to browse the web.

To see where you are on the Web, take a look at the "Location" or "Address" box near the top of the browser. If the words "www.microsoft.com" are in this box, you're looking at the Microsoft web site. You may see some words or letters before or after the www.microsoft.com address, but don't worry about them.

Now click on the "Location" or "Address" box. The entire line may become highlighted. That's normal. Press the backspace key on your keyboard, deleting all the letters that are in the box. Type the following: www.greentreepress.com. Then hit the "Enter" key on your keyboard. As your computer starts to find and display the Green Tree Press web page, you'll see several things happening. The screen will start to fill up with text and graphics. At the bottom of the screen you may see some numbers. This is all normal. Just wait for the web page to load.

When the page has finished loading, move the cursor around the web page. As you move over certain pictures or underlined words, you'll see the cursor change from a pointer into a hand with a finger pointing. This means that you can click and go to another page. You can also scroll down this page by using the scroll bar on the right side of the window. Scroll down the page until you see a row of links. You can spot links because they'll be underlined and in a different color from the rest of the text.

When you put the cursor over one of these links, it'll change into a pointing hand. When it does, click on it. A new page will load. You can now use the "Back" button on your browser to go back to the previous page. Try it now. When the previous page has loaded, click on the "Forward" button. As you can see, it takes you forward to the page you just came back from. It's one way of turning pages on a web site.

Click on the "Reload" or "Refresh" button on your browser. It does exactly what its name suggests. If you go back or forward to different pages, sometimes they don't load properly on your computer. This is because once you view a web page, your computer temporarily stores some of the page. That helps it to load faster if you return to it later. But if you're experiencing difficulties, just click on the "Reload" or "Refresh" button and the computer will get a new copy of the page from the Internet.

Click on the "Home" button on your browser. This takes you back to a specially designated web page your computer is programmed to take you to whenever this button is clicked.

IV.

Search Engines

Finding what you want on the Internet can be confusing and frustrating. Luckily, there are some good web sites out there to help you find what you're looking for. These sites are called search engines.

Probably one of the most popular search engines — Yahoo — isn't really a search engine at all. It's more of an on-line directory. Remember, you don't have to click on your browser's "Search" button to do a search. Click on the "Address" or "Location" box in your browser, type in www.yahoo.com, and press the "Enter" key on your keyboard.

Note: In fact you can go anywhere in the world this way. Just click on the "address" or "location" box and type in a URL and press enter.

After the page loads you'll see the Yahoo welcome screen. In the middle of the page is an empty white box with a "Search" button next to it. Type in what you're looking for and click on this button. Yahoo will then give you the results. But be prepared. These results may number in the thousands. If there are simply too many, just click on the "Back" button and try another search. This time, try to be a bit more specific.

Whenever you're too vague with your search request, you'll get far too many matches for you to go through. On the other hand, if you're too specific, you may not find anything at all. Experiment with a few different searches. If you ever get stuck, use the help link at the upper right hand corner of the web page.

A true search engine, such as those listed below, sends out search programs called spiders that comb (or crawl) the Internet looking for Web pages. All this information gets entered into the particular search engine's database. It's very likely that you will get different results with different search engines. Always try two or three for a good search.

Here is a list of other popular search engines:

www.google.com

www.hotbot.com

www.altavista.com

www.lycos.com

www.webcrawler.com

116

A. Free stuff

The Internet offers a lot of pure enjoyment. And some things are free! Here are some examples.

A site called www.shareware.com can give you free software. Once you go there, you can search for any type of program. All the software on www.shareware.com is free for the taking. Some of the program authors ask that you send them a small fee if you like their games or programs. The beauty of this is that you get to try the software out before you buy it.

Speaking of free, one of the leading anti-virus programs in the world is McAfee's Anti-Virus. You can get a free evaluation copy just by going to their web site at www.mcafee.com and clicking on the download link.

One cool web site is www.real.com There you can download a free real audio player that will let you listen to music and video over the Internet. There are hundreds of radio stations and some television stations on the Internet that will let you listen to them with this program. You can listen to radio literally from around the world. In stereo too.

A cool program you may find handy is at the www.icuii.com web site. This software lets you talk to anyone else with an Internet connection and the same software, just as though you were talking on the phone. The only difference is that you can talk as long as you want because there are no long distance charges.

www.dragonsys.com offers a program that lets you talk to your computer, which in turn types what you say. This is a useful program that will let you type anything from e-mail to books without ever having to know how to type. You can even use the program to help control your computer. Use your voice instead of the mouse. This program is not free, but if you need it, it's fun.

B. Local internet service

If you're using America On-Line (AOL), you've no doubt encountered busy signals when you try to connect. You can avoid this if you have a local Internet Service Provider account. You can use your local ISP to connect to the Internet and then get onto AOL without those pesky busy signals.

Connect to the Internet with your dial-up connection, explained earlier, and then double click on your AOL program. Set up your account so that AOL will use TCP/IP instead of the modem to log on. Once you do this, you'll be able to get onto AOL and the internet without ever worrying about busy signals.

This process can vary, depending upon what version of AOL you have. You may have to call AOL customer service for help.

Another more advanced technique is to have multiple e-mail accounts. This can be quite handy if you want to stop getting junk e-mail. To understand how this works you need to know a little bit about how you get junk e-mail in the first place.

When you send an e-mail out to a number of people or over a news group, you're broadcasting your e-mail address to the world. Some people have written programs to help them collect e-mail accounts. What they mail to the accounts they've gathered is considered by many people to be junk mail.

You can avoid junk mail by never giving out your e-mail address. But then why have it in the first place? The best tactic is to have a private e-mail — like a private phone line — that you give out only to your friends and family.

That way, when a newsgroup or a business asks for your e-mail address, you give them one of your "public" e-mail addresses. You can get free e-mails at many places, including one called www.hotmail.com.

Quite possibly, you can avoid junk e-mail completely at your private e-mail address.

C. Using your computer as a fax machine

If your computer came with a fax modem you should have a CD or floppy disk with the fax software that you'll need in order to install the fax modem on your computer. Once you install this software, you'll be able to send and receive faxes.

Since there are so many types of fax programs and fax modems, it's impossible here to go over each individually. Instead, let's just look at what's involved in using your computer to send a fax. Refer to the instructions that came with your specific fax software if you need to.

If you don't have a scanner on your computer, you'll be able to send faxes only of files you make on your computer. For example, you could fax a letter you typed on your computer or a picture that you drew on your computer. If you have a scanner on your computer you can scan in pictures and other documents and then send them with your fax modem.

To send a fax on your computer, you need to print the file first. Select "Print" from the program you're using to make the fax. You'll get a print window where you can select the printer to use. Click on the down arrow next to the name of the printer and select the fax modem from the list. Then click on the "Print" button.

The fax software should pop up on the screen and ask you for a phone number to send the fax to. Enter the number, click on the "Send" button, and your computer will send the fax.

To receive a fax, you'll need to have your fax software running. When the phone rings and it's a fax, click on the "manual receive" button and your computer should start receiving the fax.

D. Some more about attachments

When you are sending an e-mail message to someone, you can attach a file that will be sent along with your message. The file you attach to your e-mail can be any file that is on your computer, including photographs.

In order to attach a file you must know where the file is on your computer and what it is called. When you click on the "Attach" button on your e-mail program a window will open that will let you type in the file you want to attach. It is often best to click on the "Browse" button and locate the file by clicking on it rather than just typing in the name of the file you want to attach.

Remember that if you can't find the file you want to attach you can always use the "Find" option in Windows to help you locate it. If you aren't sure how to do this refer back to the beginning of this book where the "Find" option was covered.

Attachments are like things you include with normal correspondences. If you were sending a photograph with a hand written letter, you would simply include the picture with your letter itself. The picture would not be part of your letter, but rather a separate object you put into the envelope (an attachment).

Because of this, keep in mind that if you attach a photograph to your e-mail it may not be displayed on your screen. This is normal. It may just show up in the message window someplace in a list of attachments. Rest assured that when the person you sent the message to receives it they will get your attachment and be able to view it by simply clicking on it.

When you attach a file to your e-mail it will make your message larger and consequently it will take a little longer to send it. At the other end, your friend will notice that the message you sent them with the attachment will take longer to get off the Internet. For this reason it's usually a good idea to try to keep the size and amount of attachments you send to a minimum.

Once a friend sent me an e-mail with a very large music file attached to it. It took me over 30 minutes to get it. I had to leave my computer and watch a television show while my computer downloaded the message. I can assure you that the music he sent me was not worth the wait.

V.
Viruses

A virus is a small program that is attached to other programs. These clever little bits of computer code are smart enough to know what programs there are on your computer and how to rewrite those programs so that they will include the virus in their own program code.

While this is happening you probably won't notice anything different about your computer at all. Once the virus has finished infecting your computer, anytime you give someone a file or program on a floppy disk or send these files to a friend over the Internet, you'll be sending the virus, too.

When your friend opens the file or runs the program you sent him, the virus will also run and start infecting his computer. In a few days hundreds or even thousands of computers can become infected.

Since a virus is a program, once it is running, it can do just about anything that the creator wants it to do. Anything from displaying messages and graphics to deleting files on your computer or erasing your hard disk. A

virus, however, cannot hurt your computer hardware. There is no way for a virus to destroy your ram or motherboard. It can only make it appear as though they are not working properly. Once the virus is removed and your computer restored to factory condition everything will be back to normal.

Unfortunately, there is no way to completely protect your computer from viruses. The best that you can do is purchase or download a commercial virus protection program.

When you buy a virus protection program the manufacturer usually gives you some free upgrades and/or offers a plan that, for a small fee, will give you access to monthly or even weekly updates. Since there are new viruses created every day, even the best virus protecting program may eventually let a new virus infect your computer. It is important to keep your virus protection program current.

Computer viruses infect your computer like real viruses infect humans. Anytime your computer comes into contact with an infected computer it is possible for your computer to become infected. This can happen through floppy disks or even files given to you over the Internet. That's why it is important to always test or scan any files you are given.

Although having any virus on your computer is a bad thing, not all viruses are disastrous. We all hear the stories of the computer virus that erases all the files on your computer, but there are many other viruses that simply play tricks on you or do nothing at all.

It is possible that you may never know you have a virus on your computer. Or perhaps once a year, booting up your computer may give you a message like "Happy Birthday." After that, your computer works fine for the rest of the year.

I point this out because you should know that just because your computer seems to be running fine and has no problems, you may still have a virus and be infecting others.

VI.

How to Buy and Sell Stocks and Book Travel Reservations

The growing power and flexibility of the Internet has allowed us to change the way we buy and sell things. Today it's perfectly safe to buy products over the Internet, provided you're using a secure web site. You can tell that the web site is secure by looking for a locked padlock at the bottom of your browser.

If you want to travel, you can now book your airline tickets, hotel and even rental car all without leaving home. Most the time you'll save money too. A good strategy for buying airline tickets online is to try a couple of different web sites and then compare prices with a local travel agent. Almost always the Internet will be much less expensive for the exact same ticket.

Some travel web sites that you can try are:

1. www.travelocity.com

2. www.expedia.com

3. www.priceline.com

The first two are web sites that enable you to search for the lowest airfares and hotel rates on the dates and destinations you choose. You start out by selecting the date you want to travel and the city you wish to visit, and the web sites show you the lowest fares.

After you choose your tickets you can then check hotel rates and rental car rates. In one afternoon without leaving your home you can book a complete trip. Using these web services is fun and can save you money.

The last one on the list (www.priceline.com) is a bit different from the others. On Priceline you bid for your airline tickets. If you do use this service it's in your best interest to check the going rate for the airline tickets you want and then go to Priceline and bid what you think is a fair price.

This makes for a buyer beware situation. You agree to buy the ticket at the price you name, even if it's not the best available rate. Therefore, make sure you know the going rate for the ticket you're bidding on. Then bid a lower price.

Another thing to keep in mind with Priceline.com is that most of the tickets come with restrictions. These can range from long layovers to multiple connections.

You can get good deals with Priceline, but there's no guarantee you'll get your tickets. You'll get them only if the airline agrees to sell them to you at your price. If you don't have flexible travel plans, you'd be better off using either Travelocity or Expedia.com.

Because things change so quickly on the Internet, you may want to use a search engine to look for other web sites that sell airline tickets, book hotels, and rent cars.

Another exciting new way you can use your computer is to trade stocks online. Until recently, commission fees charged by stockbrokers for trading were very expensive. With the advent of the Internet it's now possible to trade stocks very inexpensively. It isn't uncommon to see online brokers offering trades for as low as $12 or even less.

The first thing you need to consider when choosing an online broker is reliability. Try to use a well-known name that has a good track record. You can also ask your friends what brokers they use as well. Some of the online brokers offer checking and other banking services too. Don't use stockbrokers just because they have the lowest commission.

Instead, do a little homework. Once you decide on a stockbroker, he or she will give you the information you need to use their service.

One word of caution. Trading stocks online is very quick and easy. Don't fall prey to overuse of the services. Like all things that involve money, careful consideration and perhaps professional advice should be sought before jumping in.

Some online stockbrokers you can consider:

1. www.etrade.com

2. www.tdwaterhouse.com

3. www.ameritrade.com

4. www.mydiscountbroker.com

Because the Internet changes quickly, you may want to use a search engine to look for other online brokers and to check their commissions and services.

VII.
Reminder Service

A handy website that I use is called my.excite.com and it allows you to have a personal homepage on the Internet. This is a free service that anyone can have, and it's full of useful news, information and tools. If you're interested in trying it out, use your browser to visit my.excite.com by typing the name in exactly as shown. There is no www in front of this web address.

Once you've chosen a username and a password, you can set up your homepage to track the stocks you own, to show you local weather and even to clip news headlines that fit your own personal tastes.

One tool that's particularly handy is the reminders section. Here you can add special events or appointments that you want to be reminded of.

If you use my.excite.com as your own personal homepage, I recommend that you make it the home page in your browser. If you're unsure how to do this, refer to the next section for the particular browser you use.

VIII.
Choosing a Startup or Homepage

You can choose a special startup page for your browser that automatically shows up when you run the browser or when you click on the Home button. If you want to change this option, follow these steps.

Internet Explorer

1. Click on "Tools" at the top of the window and then on "Internet Options."

2. Click on the "General" tab in the window that opens.

3. The first section of this window is titled "Home page." Type in the website address that you want the browser to use. Be sure that the web address you type in starts with http:// (i.e. if you want to use my.excite.com as you homepage type in http://my.excite.com)

4. Click on "Ok."

Netscape

1. Click on the word "Edit" in the Netscape window.

2. Click on the option "Navigator" on the left.

3. The second section on the right hand side is titled "Home page." Type in the web site address that you want the browser to use. Be sure that the web address you type in starts with http:// (i.e. if you want to use my.excite.com as you homepage type in http://my.excite.com)

4. Click on "Ok."

IX.

U.S. Naval Observatory

Have you ever wanted to know exactly what time it is? Thanks to the Internet it's possible to connect to one of the major timekeepers of the world, the United States Naval Observatory atomic clock.

To get there log onto the Internet and use your browser to visit the following web site.

tycho.usno.navy.mil

Once there you'll be shown the time of day. There is even an option to hear the atomic clock tell you the time. You can't get more precise than that.

X.

Reference Books

With the use of the Internet you can access volume upon volume of valuable information on just about anything you can think of. Often, the hard part is finding the information.

I've included a few links you may find useful.

Encyclopedias:

www.britannica.com

www.infoplease.com

www.funkandwagnalls.com

The Internet offers more than just typical encyclopedias. An example of a special subject encyclopedia on the Internet is orb.rhodes.edu that you can use if you're interested in Medieval Studies.

Dictionaries

www.webster.com

dictionary.msn.com

humanities.uchicago.edu/forms_unrest/webster.form.html

These are only a few examples of what's available on the Internet, if you want to find more just use a search engine, like www.google.com or www.yahoo.com, and do your own search for a dictionary or encyclopedia. While you're at it, try searching for "thesaurus" or some other reference book and see what you can find. You may be surprised at what's out there.

XI.

Creating Your Own Website

There's a web site that allows you to set up your own Internet business for free. The web address is http://www1.excite.com/home/info/business/business_overview/ if you're interested. This free service is a great way to try out your own ideas and see if they can make money.

This may sound too good to be true, how-ever, and there are some compromises involved. You'll have to market your business on your own and use products provided from the Excite service.

Overall, I think this is a very good service. You get to set up shop and try to sell goods over the Internet for free. If you're successful and start selling, then you'll know that you're idea works and can decide whether or not to take the next step and create your own full fledged e-business.

One benefit of using the Excite Store Builder is that there are a host of options that you get with your on-line business, including credit card transactions and shopping carts. Because this is a new service and the details can change, I recommend that you visit the web site and get all the details first hand.

If the above address doesn't work you can get the most current information about the Excite store builder from their home page at www.excite.com. Look under "Tools" and "Small Business" on their homepage.

If you aren't interested in starting an online business but just want a simple family web page, then you may be interested in visiting geocities.yahoo.com and signing up for their service.

Geocities is a place to go in order to set up your own personal web page. It's a free service. Once again, it's paid for by advertisers, so you'll have advertisements placed on your page. Still, you can put up just about anything you want on your web page without knowing much about creating web pages. Another website that lets you create your own webpages is www.fortunecity.com.

If you're interested, check out the following web sites for the most current and up-to-date information.

http://www1.excite.com/home/info/business/business_overview/

http://geocities.yahoo.com/home/

www.fortunecity.com

XII.
Instant Messaging

With instant messaging you can use your computer to send a message or chat with people around the world. AOL Instant Messenger (AIM) will let you type back and forth with another person as well as share files, drawings and photos. The latest AOL Instant Messenger (AIM) will even allow you to talk to other people as though you were on the telephone.

If you're currently using AOL as your Internet provider, then you already have AIM on your computer. If you're not an AOL customer, you can get AIM free by visiting www.aim.com and downloading it. You'll need to sign up for a user name in order to use AIM, but that's free too.

Once you download and install it you'll be able to talk to anyone else who has AIM. When they get on the Internet you'll see them appear in your AIM window and you'll be able to talk with them instantly by typing back and forth. Simply double click on their name and a window will open that lets you converse with your friend. If you want to use AIM like a phone, you'll need a computer that has both speakers and a microphone. The person you're talking with will need the same setup. Keep in mind that using AIM as a phone is fun, but many factors affect how efficiently it works. You may find that it's not as useful as using a real phone.

XIII.
Online Catalogs

There are hundreds of online catalogs that you can use for shopping. The quickest way to find them is to simply type in the name of the catalog or company you're looking for. For example, if you're looking for Lands End try typing www.landsend.com in your web browser and see if anything comes up. Many times this works fine, but when you can't find the company you're looking for, use an Internet search engine such as Yahoo or Google.

For more information on using search engines refer to the Internet section of Computer Friendly. (Page 116).

XIV.
Genealogy

If you're interested in researching your family genealogy, the Internet can be a very useful tool. One of the fist places you should visit is www.genealogy.com to start your family search. Genealogy.com lets you search your family name and set up an online family tree.

Another useful website is www.ancestry.com, which offers more search tools and tips. You can search for family names and go through several databases that may help you compile your family tree.

Keep in mind that although some of the services on these websites are free, others may charge a fee. You'll always be told if a service is going to cost money, so don't worry about being charged without your knowledge or permission.

You can also search the Internet by using search engines such as Yahoo or Google for more genealogy websites or family names. For more information on using search engines, refer to the Internet section of Computer Friendly. (Page 116).

XV.
Medical Info

A wealth of medical information is available on the Internet. Some of the best places to find information are the drug manufacturers themselves. All of the major drug companies have websites, and you can find them by using a search engine or by simply typing the company's name — or perhaps a drug name — into your web browser. Be sure to type the company name or drug name into your browser using the www. — .com format, where — is the name of the company or drug you're looking for.

Two websites that you may find helpful for medical information are www.webmd.com and www.mayoclinic.com. Each of these websites offers information on various medical topics. At the www.webmd.com website, just type in a few words describing what you're looking for and then view the search results. The world renowned Mayo Clinic website lets you search for medical information on various topics from diseases to medication and treatments.

Lesson Six

YOUR FINAL PROJECTS

H ere are several projects that will test your ability to apply what you've learned. See how many you can do without going back to your previous lessons.

I've tried to make them as practical as possible given the fact that I don't know you personally.

Project #1

Assume that you're bored with the standard background on your screen. You're also bored with your current screen saver ... even the size of your icons and the fonts you're using.

Can you change them? How?

Project #2

Here are some handy folders that most everyone would like to have. See if you can create a few for yourself.

1. Christmas and other holiday names and addresses.

First, sort them by holiday. Who sent you cards? Then categorize them into sub folders dividing them into business, family and friends (which might be handy for tax purposes)?

2. Tax records: Why not begin organizing all deductible expenses by individual deductions and by month? Now, come tax time, you don't have to rack your brain for deductions.

3. House and home records — especially with reference to what you purchase and when? A new furnace? New screens? A new TV? A new lawn tractor? What were the conditions set forth in the warranties? Where are the actual warranties kept?

Project #3

Go to www.shareware.com and look for programs you might enjoy. Choose a game you might find appealing. Then, see what other types of programs you can find.

Project #4

Go to www.yahoo.com and see if you can find a place in Scotland where you can purchase beautiful sweaters. Shopping is both unique and fun on the Internet.

Project #5

Go to www.altavista.com and see if you can uncover all the little-known facts about a prescription drug you or someone you know may be taking.

Project #6

Your computer has a basic word processor called "WordPad." You can run it by clicking on the "Start" button, then putting the pointer over the word "Programs." Now, move the pointer over the "Accessories" option. Then click on the WordPad program.

When you do this, a window will open up that will look similar to the one below.

You can select what the type will look like by changing the font in the font window and you can change the size of the letters by choosing the point size. See the figures below.

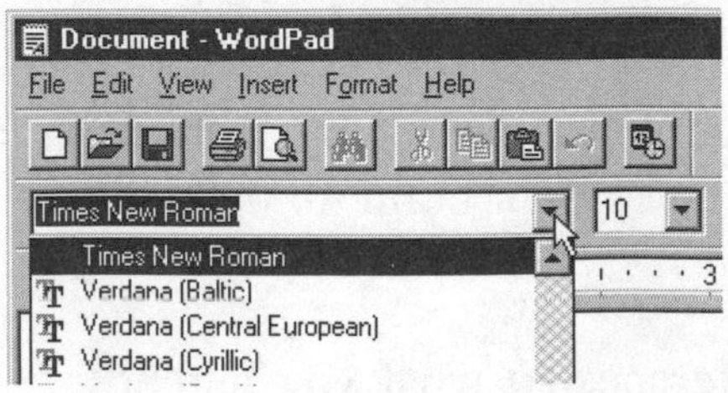

Selecting the font

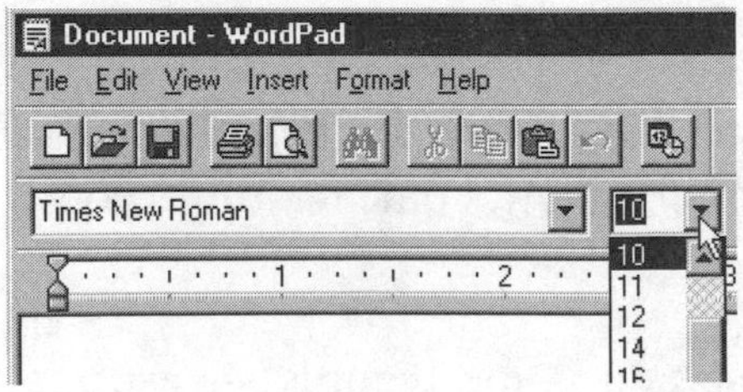

Selecting the point size

You can also place tabs by clicking on the ruler where you want to place the tab. If you want to change the placement of the tab, just click and drag it to a new section. If you want to remove a tab, just click on it and drag it off the ruler.

If you want to make text **bold,** *italic,* or <u>underlined</u>, you can do that by using the buttons on the toolbar. See the figure below.

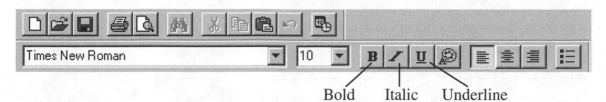

Bold   Italic   Underline

You can also change the justification, margin and line indenting by clicking on the word "Format" at the top of the window and selecting the "Paragraph" option.

When you are finished you can print the file by clicking on the printer button near the top of the window.

ANSWERS TO EXERCISES

Exercise One Answers

1. Cards
2. Word processor
3. CD-ROM Drive
4. Monitor
5. Floppy disk
6. Hard disk
7. CPU
8. Keyboard
9. CD-ROM
10. Sound card
11. Microphone
12. Modem
13. Motherboard
14. Programs
15. Software
16. Scanner
17. Printer
18. Speakers
19. Video card
20. Disk drive
21. Mouse

Exercise Two Answers

1. B
2. C
3. B
4. A

Exercise Three Answers

1. Operating System   2. Icons   3. Cursor   4. The "Start" button and the clock

Exercise Four Answers

1. A folder   2. Open (execute or run also correct)   3. Drag the icon around the screen   4. Double click

5. Execute (open also correct)   6. Close it   7. A file   8. Application

Exercise Five Answers

1. A gadget
2. Input (or inputting)
3. Install
4. Launch
5. Left click
6. Load
7. Maximize
8. Minimize

Exercise Six Answers

1. Save
2. Restore
3. Right click
4. Scroll bar(s)
5. Menu
6. Run
7. Shortcut

Exercise Seven Answers

1. Windows   2. Shut down   3. Task bar   4. Start button   5. Title bar

Exercise Eight Answers

1. B   2. C   3. A   4. D

Name the parts of this window...

1. Minimize, maximize and close gadgets   2. List of folders and files   3. Current location or path
4. Commands and options   5. Title bar

Exercise Nine Answers

1. Left click once on it   2. Double click on it (with left button)   3. C: 4. A:

Exercise Twelve Answers

Shut Down: If you are turning your computer off for the day.

Restart: If you feel that your computer is not acting properly, or if you just installed new software.

Stand By: If your just going to leave your computer for a few hours.

Exercise Thirteen Answer

Windows organizes information on your hard drive and other disks by using files and folders. You can place files into folders and have as many folders within a folder as you want. This way you can organize the files and folders any way you want.

Exercise Fourteen Answers

1. Save in: the place your file will be put   2. Up one level
3. Create new folder   4. File list box
5. File name: the name you want the file to be called   6. Save as type

Internet Section

Exercise One Answers

1. Book marks   2. News groups   3. Tone dialing   4. Connect
5. ISDN   6. Download   7. Call waiting   8. E-commerce
9. Link   10. Modem   11. Hyperlink (or just link)   12. Internet
13. ISP   14. Password   15. Login or Logon   16. ADSL
17. Pulse dial   18. Dial up   19. TCP/IP   20. E-mail
21. URL   22. Username